Austin Boulevard:

The Invisible Line between

Two Worlds

By Jeff Ferdinand

Austin Boulevard

Copyright 2017 Jeff Ferdinand

ISBN: 978-1539302278

Printed in the United States of America.

Table of Contents

A Word from the Author

This book is about race in America. More specifically, it is about the long and dark history of racial discrimination against African-Americans in the United States. I use Austin Boulevard, a street dividing Oak Park and the neighborhood of Austin Village in Chicago, as a metaphor for the divide that exists between black and white, rich and poor, privileged and unprivileged.

Austin Boulevard is a street that I lived on for two years. During that time, my experiences inspired me to write about the stark differences of living on one side of the street versus the other. I wanted to learn more about the two neighborhoods I straddled and how they got to be the way they are today. Some of what I researched I already knew, but a lot of the information I found helped me understand how we got to be such a racially divided country.

Today, we are at a crossroads. On the surface we seem like a society that is more tolerant and accepting. And it is true that we have made great progress in becoming a more racially equal country. But under the surface we are still a society that has a tremendous amount of inequality, racial and otherwise. We have seen cities like Ferguson and Baltimore erupt in racial unrest. This tells us, along with many other factors discussed in this book that we still have a long way to go in achieving racial equality in America.

Throughout this book I intertwine my own experiences living on Austin Boulevard and working on the West Side of Chicago, with the history of blacks in America. I discuss topics such as slavery, the Great Migration, convict leasing and peonage, lynching, Jim Crow, housing segregation, the Civil Rights Movement, the war on drugs, mass incarceration, and police brutality and try to dismiss many myths we have about African-Americans.

I am writing this book from the perspective of a white male who grew up in a predominately white, middle-class suburb of Chicago. My unique experiences, as well as my knowledge of black history, have helped me write a book that is hopefully entertaining and informative. The resources I have used to gather information used in this book include many brilliant authors, journalists, activists, and historians. At the very least, I hope that you gain a new perspective on both the history and the current state of black Americans. I hope you enjoy the book!

Jeff Ferdinand

June 2016

Foreword

My thinking continues to expand through new research and experiences that I have gained in the one year since I originally published my book, Austin Boulevard: The Invisible Line between Two Worlds. I have read many new books, conducted research on the 9th floor of the Harold Washington Library in Chicago, and interviewed many people who have enhanced my knowledge and perspective of black history and how it relates to Oak Park and Austin. I have wrote a new foreword and afterword, added relevant information about Oak Park and Austin, and made revisions on historical and grammatical inaccuracies that I have found. I hope you enjoy!

What is going on in Chicago?

During Donald Trump's 2016 presidential campaign, he frequently used the violence in Chicago to gain support for his Law and Order agenda. Chicago most definitely has problems, but it also has the potential for positive change. Although politicians use violence in Chicago as well as cities around the country to further divide issues along party lines, this is not a political platform. This should be a wake up call for everyone to come together against poverty, prejudice and injustice.

In 2016, there were 762 homicides in Chicago, which was about 300 more homicides than the previous year. In fact, it was about 300 more than the combined average of the 10 previous years. On one end, it is painfully troubling that Chicago murders increased by almost 300 from 2015 to 2016. But the fact is, that the homicide rate in Chicago has declined significantly after the 1990's. This is hardly the picture the media paints. You would have thought that violence in Chicago and around the country has been getting worse and worse. The truth, however, is that violence has declined in cities throughout the United States significantly in the last 16 or 17 years. Also, many people suggest that Chicago is the nation's murder capital. This is far from the truth. Homicides cannot be compared based on a total number due to the differences in populations from city to city. To compare the deadliest cities, you would have to compare the murder rate of each city. The murder rate counts murders per 100,000 residents. When taken this into account, Chicago is not even close to the murder capital of the United States.

I have been to many discussions in Chicago's most violent neighborhoods and rarely are gun control and the addition of more police officers a main topic of discussion. Yet, this is all we hear in the news. Many residents of these neighborhoods voice their concerns about the lack of employment opportunities and affordable housing, healthier food options, and better schools. Yet, they get more police occupying their neighborhoods, foreclosures, and local schools being shut down. And when the violence doesn't subside, the black and brown people in these neighborhoods are blamed. It can't possibly be a lack of opportunities and resources they say, it must be that the residents of these neighborhoods aren't taking responsibility for their actions. Or they say that the residents in these communities aren't working hard enough, or there are not enough positive role models and devoted parents.

In a speech given by Keeanga-Yamahtta Taylor in response to the election of Donald Trump, she gives a counter-narrative to the typical explanations for the persistent violence in Chicago. She says, "What is almost never offered as at least part of the answer [to Chicago's violence] is how Chicago has the highest black unemployment rate of the nation's five largest cities at 25 percent, that nearly half of black men aged 20 to 24 are neither in school nor employed, that Chicago has the third-highest poverty rate of large cities in the US, and that it is the most segregated city in the country."

When we blame bad parenting, a lack of personal responsibility, 'a culture of violence', and poor role models for the violence that is plaguing Chicago's West and South Sides, we are distracting ourselves from the real solutions that can lead to long-term, meaningful change. We are also, perhaps intentionally or unintentionally, rationalizing the violence through the racist ideas that black people are somehow inferior parents, too lazy to get and keep jobs, and are more prone to violence than others.

This is not to say that the criminals that are perpetrating this violence should not be held accountable. In fact, far too many are not being held accountable, which in turn is perpetuating the cycle of violence. Despite the fact that we are the world's largest jailer and Chicago contributes to this fact considerably, the Chicago Police have a terribly low rate of bringing killers to justice. This speaks to the lack of trust between the police and the communities they serve on Chicago's West and South Sides, amongst many other factors.

When we talk about Chicago and the seemingly unending violence in this city, we need to stay focused on the root causes, and then we can start to come up with solutions. These root causes being economic, housing, health, and educational inequality, to name a few. There are many racial inequalities that exist in Chicago. The Institute for Research on Race and Public Policy found that in Chicago:

- ✓ Blacks are more than four times more likely to be unemployed than whites
- ✓ Over 30% of black families are below the poverty line compared to less than 10% of white families
- ✓ Black median family income is about $36,000, when white family income is almost $82,000
- ✓ Far more whites own homes than blacks and the average worth of a home for a white household is almost double that of a black household
- ✓ Chicago Public Schools in predominately black areas have far fewer educational resources and opportunities as schools in predominately white areas
- ✓ For the past 30 years, the black mortality rate is 130 times higher than the white rate
- ✓ Police are nine and a half times more likely to use excessive force against Black Chicagoans compared to White Chicagoans.

Most people would agree that there are significant racial disparities in Chicago and throughout the country, but contribute these disparities to black inferiority instead of our current and historic legacy of racial discrimination in this city and country. If our current narrative focuses on blaming black people for the current racial inequities that they face in Chicago and throughout the country, we will never be able to accurately and effectively diminish these inequalities. This will in turn lead to new ways to discriminate against African Americans. The negative results caused by the new means of discrimination will further be rationalized by racist ideas.

Making Connections

My book Austin Boulevard: The Invisible Line between Two Worlds is not a comprehensive history or oral history of the suburb of Oak Park or the Austin neighborhood. I use Austin Boulevard to illustrate the history of how the city of Chicago and the United States became racially divided and how we can become a more just and unified society.

Throughout my book, I discuss the history of slavery, convict leasing, lynching, Jim Crow, The Great Migration, housing discrimination, mass incarceration, and police brutality. Although many of these subjects may seem like history and not relevant now, I hope the reader will see that understanding this history is the very basis of understanding how to solve the problems. In the next few pages, I hope I can further help articulate the many connections between the past racial history of this country and how it relates to what is going on today.

Bryan Stevenson, the founder of Equal Justice Initiative, believes that "Slavery didn't end in 1865, it just evolved." This is a crucially important way to look at the racial history of the United States. We have a tendency to use racial progress to blind us from the discrimination that is still so pervasive in this country. This is not to say that we have not made great strides to make this country a more racially inclusive place, but we should not let the idea of racial progress make us complacent with the current racial state in the United States. America has a way of adapting discrimination and fooling the public into thinking black people are responsible for the racial inequities that this discrimination is causing. Furthermore, it is critical that we see how discrimination and racism evolves, so we can then better stop it when it attempts to change its form.

We still need to talk about slavery. We need to talk about it in a way that does not romanticize it. When we give a watered down version of slavery, it allows us to alter the history that slavery created. Slavery created a narrative that African Americans are an inferior race. This was created to justify enslaving human beings. Those who participated in the slave industry convinced themselves and others that they were actually helping their slaves by providing for them, and because blacks could not handle freedom, they were actually doing them a favor. This narrative would evolve and justify many other forms of discrimination.

Slavery, of course, was an extremely profitable business for the South and the North. When the Civil War ended and slaves gained their freedom, the South found new ways to provide free labor at the expense of black bodies. Slavery then evolved into sharecropping and convict leasing. Those who benefited from this free labor, continued to justify it by the same racist ideas of black inferiority. Today, prison labor and prisons themselves enrich corporations and create jobs.

In her book The New Jim Crow, Michelle Alexander explains how many of us justify locking up millions of black and brown people. "The genius of the current caste system, and what most distinguishes it from its predecessors, is that it appears voluntary. People choose to commit crimes, and that's why they are locked up or locked out, we are told. This feature makes the politics of responsibility particularly tempting, as it appears the system can be avoided with good behavior. But herein lies the trap. All people make mistakes. All of us are sinners. All of us are criminals. All of us violate the law at some point in our lives." The stereotype that African Americans are more prone to criminality and are a danger to society allows us to discriminatorily lock them up at disproportionate rates, even when studies show that, for instance, white and black people use and sell drugs at similar rates. We have used the war on drugs to target and incarcerate a truly extraordinary amount of black and Latino men and women for minor drug violations. This is the same tactic used by the South when law enforcement would target blacks for vagrancy, loitering, talking too loud, and a plethora of other meaningless and discriminatory laws. When viewed from this perspective, we should understand that mass incarceration is yet just another evolution of slavery.

We should also make connections between housing discrimination now and then. As blacks started migrating north to cities like Chicago, they had a difficult time securing housing. Redlining segregated them into ghettos and they were not allowed to purchase mortgages, striping them from accumulating wealth the way so many white families were able to. Blockbusting and panic peddling added to the isolation of black ghettos. When whites fled, so did businesses and any hope of economic development Not only did this create the ghettos that still persist today in Chicago and throughout the country, but this segregation continues to make it easier for blacks to be discriminated against. African Americans are far more likely than whites to be targeted with subprime mortgages. According to many studies, black households lost about half of their wealth during the great recession when so many families, of all colors, were affected by subprime loans. Blacks, however, were affected the most, losing more wealth than any other racial group.

The United States has a long and violent history of restricting the black vote. Slaves, of course, could not vote. When they did gain the franchise, the South quickly moved to suppress black people from gaining any political power. Voting requirements such as land ownership, literacy tests, and poll taxes all affected black voters disproportionately. Today, felony disenfranchisement, gerrymandering, and voter ID laws are responsible for eliminating or limiting the ability of millions of black and latino people to vote.

When laws and policies were not enough to keep blacks marginalized, violence was used. Whether it was slave patrols, lynchings, housing riots, or police brutality, whites have rarely faced accountability for vigilante violence. It is not lost on black people, when they see Michael Brown's body lying dead in the street for hours, that the destruction of black bodies have been used to intimidate and control the progression of African-Americans.

It may be cliché to say that if we don't know our history, we are doomed to repeat it; but it is often painfully evident from generation to generation. Those with power are always susceptible to use it to maintain and enhance their privilege through any means necessary. It is our job to promptly identify this, and then resist!

Jeff Ferdinand
August, 2017

Acknowledgments

I would like to thank my editor Kathleen Tracy for sharpening and improving my work, Nancy Valladolid for bringing my book to life with her moving photographs, and my mother, Sharon Ferdinand, for beautifully designing the cover. I am grateful for the support from my family and wife, Elise. A special thanks to everyone who I interviewed including Jo-Anne Willis, Rob Breymaier, Ethan Michaeli, Rasha Myers, Erick Paige, and Pierre Mahone.

I would also like to thank all of the authors, journalists, and historians whose work I referenced in this book. Your work has educated and inspired me to write this book.

Austin Boulevard

Introduction

~Don't make eye contact.

I was driving my dark gray, Honda Insight like it was my first time driving. I had my hands on 10 and 2 and was hyper aware of my surroundings. My head was on a swivel, foot riding the break, going slower than a 90-year-old driving an old Cadillac. There were small beads of sweat on my forehead, and my body felt like I was bracing for a head on collision. (Keep in mind I was probably going no more than 15 miles per hour). Where was I? I was driving on Austin Boulevard, on the border of Oak Park and the Austin neighborhood of Chicago...

My wife and I had needed a new place to live. The end of our lease was closing in and there was no particular neighborhood we wanted to live in. I came up with the idea of looking for apartments in Oak Park, Illinois; a middle to upper class suburban neighborhood straddling the West Side of Chicago. Even though my wife and I knew no one living there, and it was farther from my job, we decided to go and check it out. As we drove around Oak Park looking at apartments, we both were fairly certain that we were going to make this our new home. The only question giving us pause was, is it safe? Well, more specifically, was the area that we could afford safe?

Driving east on Washington Boulevard, we decided to head into uncharted territory. We were not entering into another county or state, and definitely not another country, but it certainly felt like it. As we passed Austin Boulevard, we entered an entirely new world known as Austin, located on the far west side of Chicago. As sweat glazed my face, I locked the doors once, then twice. As I looked around all I saw was black faces. I heard yelling. I was sure it was being directed towards me. Was I breaking some rule I was unaware of? Were they yelling at my wife and me because we were white? Did we overstep our boundaries?

As my anxiety skyrocketed my wife demanded, "Don't make eye contact." She's right, I thought to myself. Just look straight ahead. It'll be fine. I assured myself that we were not going to get robbed or shot as I beelined it back to Oak Park. As soon as we crossed Austin Boulevard back into Oak Park, my anxiety level started to go down. I sat back in my seat, unlocked the doors, and starting driving the speed limit again.

Why did I react like that? I was not driving down an unpaved road in Baghdad amidst an air strike with foreigners aiming AK-47s at my face. I was in Chicago. The city I knew. The city I was born in. Why did I feel like I was one stare away from needing to change my underwear? Why was I so scared? I've seen black people before. I've spent time in poor neighborhoods.

That was my initial response. But soon I had other questions. Why was there such intense segregation, when segregation was declared unconstitutional more than 50 years ago? Why are there multi-million dollar mansions on one side of Austin Boulevard and vacant houses with boards covering all the windows and doors on the other side of the street? We are constantly told that we live in the best country in the world, the home of equality and opportunity. I starting wondering: Is the United States the best country in the world? Maybe it is...but for whom?

As my wife and I contemplated whether to live on Austin Boulevard, the time on our lease was closing in. We talked about it, weighed the pros and cons, and started asking around what life would be like living on Austin Boulevard. Although there were some mixed feelings, the overall consensus was a resounding no! People told us it was unsafe, that we would get robbed or attacked, and that we could not walk around at night.

The list went on.

We asked these same people if they had ever lived on Austin Boulevard, or even stepped inside the Austin neighborhood. The answer was always no. We were then able to get in contact with people who actually had experienced living on or near Austin Boulevard. Their answers to our questions were considerably different. These people told us that they had lived on Austin Boulevard for many years and never felt unsafe. It was the assurance we needed. We decided to move in.

The Invisible Line

~The division between good and bad.

I once told someone that I lived on Austin Boulevard. Their response was, "Oh, Austin Boulevard, the division between good and bad."

I smiled, chuckled a little bit, and then quickly changed the subject. Soon after, this quote came back to me. I thought about it for a while, but could not tell if it bothered me or not. My wife and I have had many encounters with people degrading an area they barely know. After my wife told someone that she lived on Austin Boulevard, they responded: "Oh, you poor thing," like she was a sick dog. So I was somewhat used to such comments—and there was definitely some truth to them.

Oak Park is a middle to upper-class neighborhood with great schools, thriving businesses, and safety. Tourists come to see the architecture of Frank Lloyd Wright. It is the home of Ernest Hemingway. But Austin is a poor neighborhood, with failing schools and businesses, dilapidated housing, gangs, and crime. So I guess this person was correct in saying that Austin Boulevard is a division between good and bad, right?

But what do we mean by bad? Are we concluding that all the people in Austin are bad? Are we condemning a whole community? Are we saying that the entire Austin neighborhood is a wasteland and has no hope?

\#

To really understand the dynamics of this invisible wall dividing good and bad, we have to take a look back in time. Oak Park and Austin started off as part of Cicero Township, which was organized in 1857, and built in 1871 near Austin Boulevard and Lake Street. Originally, English and native born Americans inhabited Cicero's Western Border and people of German, Irish, Scandinavian, and Polish ancestry lived near its Northern Boundary. Weak political leadership and the extension of the Lake Street Line to Austin Boulevard caused the splitting of Cicero Township. Oak Park and Berwyn declared their independence from Cicero and Austin was annexed to Chicago in 1889. These separate towns would each take their own unique trajectories. Oak

Park would become famous for its integration and diversity. Cicero and Berwyn acquired a reputation for racial intolerance. Cicero gained its notoriety as the headquarters of Al Capone, the 1951 race riots that captured national attention, and its political corruption. Crime, gangs, and neglect became synonymous with the West Side community of Austin. However, this was not the beginning of the invisible wall known as Austin Boulevard.

Austin's residential growth increased for years after its annexation as the population grew to 130,000 leading up to the Great Depression. The community of Austin flourished for the first half of the twentieth century. Katie Kather, the author of the article "Austin Boulevard: The Invisible Barbed Wire," explains: "Out on the far West Side of the city, 25 minutes by [the] L from the noise, dirt, and aloofness of the loop [sic] lies one of the largest hobby centers in the nation, Austin Town Hall at 5610 Lake St. Here in the heart of the Austin community, more than 150 types of hobbies and activities are centered. Attendance is impossible to estimate since groups meet every hour of the day and evening of the week."[1]

Much like Austin, Oak Park thrived after splitting from Cicero. Residential growth and population increased significantly during the next half century. Many of the current building in Oak Park were built during this time. The many modes of transportation and Oak Park's proximity to the city made it an ideal place to live. Oak Park reached its peak population at about 64,000 during this time. Both Oak Park and Austin remained overwhelmingly white until the mid-1960s for Austin and slightly later for Oak Park.

As African-Americans continued to move to the West Side of Chicago from the South Side, racial turmoil began to rear its ugly head. In 1960, there were only 31 African-Americans living in Austin. By the end of the decade that number raised to 41,583. In the 1970s, over 50,000 white people moved out of Austin and 60,000 black people moved into the neighborhood. That trend continued through the next couple of decades.

The Great Migration from 1910 to 1970 was the mass movement of black Americans from the Jim Crow South to the North. Its effects on the history of the United States were drastic. In Isabel Wilkerson's fascinating book, *The Warmth of Other Suns*, she describes the Great Migration's immense influence as "a turning point in history. It would transform urban America and recast the social and political order of every city it touched. It would force the South to search its soul and finally to lay aside a feudal caste system. It grew out of the unmet promises made after the Civil War and, through the sheer weight of it, helped push the country toward the civil rights revolutions of the 1960s."[3]

The Great Migration was unique because throughout history migrants generally tended to travel shorter distances. However, African-Americans during the Great Migration journeyed great lengths to find a new home. Many went from Louisiana or Texas all the way to California. Others fled Mississippi for Detroit or Chicago. Still others escaped Georgia and Florida for New York and Philadelphia.

Wilkerson described it this way: "They traveled deep into far-flung regions of their own country and in some cases clear across the continent. Thus the Great Migration had more in common with the vast movements of refugees from famine, war, and genocide in other parts of the world, where oppressed people, whether fleeing twenty-first-century Darfur or nineteenth-century Ireland, go great distances, journey across rivers, deserts, and oceans or as far as it takes to reach safety with the home that life will be better wherever they land."[4]

Although there was no famine or war in the South at the time of the Great Migration, African-Americans' desperation to break free from the shackles of Southern oppression was so profound that they left family, friends, and life as they knew it to go North into a completely foreign land. More than six million black Americans fled from the South to the North in hopes of a better life.

Wilkerson, referring to this mass migration of Black Americans, says,

"They did what human beings looking for freedom, throughout history, have often done. They left."[5]

Many left by rail line. Some of these routes were the same paths that that the migrants' ancestors took to escape slavery, which became known as the Underground Railroad. The tracks of these rail lines explain why many black Chicagoans' ancestors came from Mississippi, New York blacks from Florida, and California's blacks from Texas. Many migrants traveled North carrying nothing but the clothes on their back, for they were fleeing from a lynch mob, an irate employer, or the mere threat of impending violence. Others simply had had enough discrimination or lack of opportunities and decided it was worth the chance to venture North for the possibility of a better life.

Many left the racism and discrimination of the South in search of employment. Job opportunities were plentiful thanks to the manufacturing demands of World War I and World War II. But because blacks were desperate for work, it made them easy targets for exploitation.

In *The Warmth of Other Suns*, Wilkerson says, "According to the Harvard immigration scholar Stanley Lieberson, a major difference between the acceptance and thus life outcomes of black migrants from the South and their white immigrant counterparts was this: white immigrants and their descendants could escape the disadvantages of their station if they chose to, while that option did not hold for the vast majority of black migrants and their children." Wilkerson also states that "blacks were the lowest paid of all the recent arrivals. In 1950, blacks in the North and West made a median annual income of $1,628, compared to Italian immigrants, who made $2, 295, Czechs, who made $2,339, Poles, who made $2,419, and Russians, who made $2,717."[6]

Black migrant women had it even worse than men. Women in general were discriminated against in the workforce, which made black women the lowest in the economic hierarchy. Virtually the only jobs they could obtain were as servants, which was not all that different from employment in the South.

African-American migrant men were more likely to acquire a job, but worked under inhumane conditions, were paid unlivable wages, and were often used as strikebreakers. Ironically, Wilkerson points out that despite assumptions of Northern whites, blacks "had more education than even the northern white population they joined. The percentage of postwar black migrants who had graduated from high school was as high as or higher than that of native whites in New York, Cleveland, Philadelphia, and St. Louis and close to the percentage of whites in Chicago."[7]

The employment that blacks were able to gain, however, did not last. As World War I and then World War II came to a close, many blacks and other minorities lost their jobs. Economic hardships were not the only challenge that blacks had to overcome. Blacks were subjected to housing discrimination at the hands of predatory real estate agents and lenders. The federal government's policies only further led to the discrimination that blacks were met with as they moved north.

As blacks were forced into certain areas of cities by design, whites began to flee urban areas for the suburbs, known as *white flight*. Soon, cities in the north became increasingly segregated and filled with blacks. Real estate agencies intentionally tried to scare whites out of their neighborhoods, so they could sell their property to blacks for higher prices, called peddling or blockbusting.

Another strategy was called redlining, the practice of denying services, such as mortgage loans, to residents of certain areas based on the racial or ethnic makeups of those neighborhoods. Property owners could also legally prohibit minorities from seeing their property as they were trying to sell. Chicago was amongst the worst in this practice.

The rapid growth of black migrants caused much racial animosity. According to Hana Layson and Kenneth Warren in their article "Chicago and The Great Migration, 1915-1950,"

> Chicago became one of the most important destinations for members of the Great Migration. By the end of the nineteenth century, the city had a large population of European immigrants. In 1890 three-quarters of the city's population was a first- or second-generation immigrant, that is, they or their parents had been born in another country.

21

African-Americans made up less than 2 percent of the city. These demographics changed rapidly during the first half of the twentieth century. The black population in Chicago more than doubled during World War I to around 100,000. By 1970, as the Great Migration drew to a close, there were one million African-Americans in Chicago, a third of the city's population.[8]

Most of these blacks settled in the South Side of Chicago, which became known as the Black Belt of Chicago, and then slowly drifted towards the West Side of the city. As blacks attempted to move to white areas, landlords would increase the rent in these areas significantly.

"New Arrivals often paid twice the rent charged the whites they had just replaced for worn-out ill-kept housing,"[9] Wilkerson explains. She also cites a 1924 National Urban League study that stated, "Colored renters paid from forty to sixty [sic] percent higher rents than white tenants for the same class of apartment."[10]

Chicago, like many other northern cities affected greatly by the Great Migration, tried to limit the number of blacks migrating there. "In 1950, city aldermen and housing officials proposed restricting 13,000 new public housing units to people who had lived in Chicago for two years,"[11] Wilkerson reported.

But there was no stopping the mass exodus of African-Americans.

In northern cities affected by the Great Migration, many whites became angry that blacks were moving into "their" neighborhoods and taking "their" jobs. Wilkerson describes how the "arrival of colored migrants set off remarkable displays of hostility, ranging from organized threats against white property owners who might sell or rent to blacks to firebombing of houses before the new colored owners could even move in."[12]

Bombings became increasingly popular in the North as ways to intimidate blacks from moving into or near white neighborhoods. In Chicago, "there were fifty-eight bombings of houses that blacks moved into or were about to move into between 1917 and 1921 alone,"[13] Wilkerson recounts.

Full-out, devastating, and violent riots broke out in many cities including East St. Louis, Tulsa, Omaha, Detroit, and Chicago. As historian Isabel Wilkerson writes, "Contrary to modern assumptions, for much of the history of the United States...riots were often carried out by disaffected whites against groups perceived as threats to their survival. Thus riots would become to the North what lynchings were to the South, each a display of uncontained rage by put-upon people directed toward the scapegoats of their condition."[14]

This violence carried out by whites was generally a result of fear and pre-conceived prejudices against the black migrants entering their neighborhoods.

As discussed earlier, whites believed that African-Americans would bring down property values, justifying the harsh resistance of allowing blacks to live in their neighborhoods. But, Wilkerson notes, "Contrary to conventional wisdom, the decline in property values and neighborhood prestige was a by-product of the fear and tension itself, sociologists found. The decline often began, they noted, in barely perceptible ways, before the first colored buyer moved in."[15]

Therefore, it wasn't the black migrants who lowered property values when and after they moved in, but the anxiety the idea of integration posed amongst whites.

In 1919, tensions in Chicago broke out into a full-on race riot. On a hot day in July, a 17-year-old black boy named Eugene Williams went swimming in Lake Michigan. Eugene crossed an imaginary racial line that outraged a group of white boys, who pelted Eugene with rocks, causing him to drown.

When police arrived on the scene, blacks pointed out the perpetrators but the police refused to arrest them. This infuriated blacks and eventually led to rioting. The situation grew so out of control that the state militia was called in. After a week of rampage and disorder the unrest finally subsided, but only after 38 fatalities (23 black, 15 white), more than 500 injured, and at least one hundred left homeless.

Knowing the racial history of Chicago explains why the city currently has so many issues. The hyper-segregation that exists today in Chicago is borne from the racial strains that arose due to the Great Migration. It is easier to comprehend how an invisible barrier like Austin Boulevard can separate two radically different worlds. If whites today chose a more accepting path, Chicago would likely be a very different city.

#

In his groundbreaking book *Sundown Towns: A Hidden Dimension of American Racism*, James W. Loewen defines a sundown town as "any organized jurisdiction that for decades kept African-Americans or other groups from living in it and was thus all-white on purpose."[16]

The term *sundown town* refers to signs posted in certain communities that stated people of color had to leave the town by sundown, as in: *Niggers, don't let the sun go down on you in this town*, a warning to blacks that they would likely be met with violence if they stuck around.

Perhaps the most effective way to dispel and keep African-Americans out of towns was either violence or the threat of it. Loewen notes, "Across America, at least 50 towns, and probably many more than that, drove out their African- American populations violently. At least 16 did so in Illinois alone."[17]

Racist whites would bomb, lynch, or intimidate blacks to maintain or create all-white neighborhoods. As discussed before, many riots initiated by racist whites succeeded in their intentions to expel all blacks from a town. Once towns went all-white, the mere reputation of the town, kept blacks from going anywhere near that location.

Violence was not the only way whites kept black from integrating their neighborhoods. Many towns passed ordinances that prohibited African- Americans from being within city limits after sundown. Other laws prohibited selling or renting property to blacks.

It's a common misconception that towns are mostly white or black based on an individual's preference to live with their own race. Although this is certainly true in some instances, it cannot explain the extreme racial segregation that is evident in many areas today. James Loewen looked at many towns throughout the United States and argues their racial composition is no accident.

Before sundown towns, there were sundown states. Prior to the Civil War many states, including Illinois, passed laws that prohibited free blacks to migrate to their state. Although these laws would soon change with the temporary improvement of race relations during the Reconstruction, the relationship between whites and blacks would deteriorate greatly starting in 1890. The establishment of the Jim Crow laws in the South and the overall increasing racism throughout the country led to all-white towns.

By and large, African-Americans resided mostly in rural areas prior to the twentieth century. Even before the Great Migration, the systematic expulsion of blacks also contributed to changing demographics in the urban North's inner cities.

Loewen explains, "Whites were already driving African-Americans from small towns across the Midwest before those towns experienced any substantial migration from the South."[18]

Indeed, Illinois has a rich history with this type of discrimination. In 1940, restrictive covenants were used in more than 80 percent of Chicago and that percentage was thought to be even higher in the suburbs.[19] The federal government was implicit in this as well. The Federal Housing Administration (FHA) discouraged racial mixing in neighborhoods, citing that it would create instability. They also denied blacks from obtaining mortgages, amongst other regular housing discrimination practices.

It is common knowledge that this type of oppression and discrimination has occurred in the past down South. But more disturbing is that sundown towns are predominantly located in the North and some still exist today, not only in rural areas but are prevalent in suburbs as well. Loewen explains that urbanites formed many suburbs to control the racial composition of their town. The suburbs of Chicago were no exception.

"Just four African-American families entered any of the white suburbs of Chicago in 1961-62 combined. By 1970, exclusion was so complete that fewer than 500 black families lived in white suburban neighborhoods in the entire Chicago metropolitan area, and most of those were in just five or six suburbs.... By 1980, of Chicago's 285 suburbs, 9 [sic] had populations 30 to 50 percent black, while 117 were less than 1 percent black."[20]

Cicero and Berwyn, suburban towns just west of the Chicago near Oak Park and Austin, have a long history of white supremacy and racism. However,

25

it is less recognized that Kenilworth, a North Shore suburb of Chicago and one of the richest areas in the nation, started as a sundown town. Loewen describes how Joseph Sears, Kenilworth's developer, created covenants that restricted African- Americans from living there.[21]

In 2016, there were seven blacks living in Kenilworth. That is 0.3 percent of the population. Even towns that are now known for their racial tolerance, like Oak Park, was once a sundown suburb. In 1949, Percy Julian and his family were the first African-Americans to move into Oak Park. Julian was a respected and prestigious chemist, yet this was not enough to avoid discrimination in the all- white suburb. The town refused to turn on the water at the Julian's house, they received many threats, and there was even an attempt to burn down their house.

It should be no surprise, after knowing the dark history of sundown towns, the Great Migration, and widespread housing discrimination, that we are experiencing such high levels of residential segregation across the country, especially in cities like Chicago.

#

In the mid-1940s, African-Americans started moving out of the Black Belt on the South Side of Chicago and into the predominantly Jewish, West Side neighborhood of North Lawndale. North Lawndale is located just south of East and West Garfield park and southwest of Austin. North Lawndale began to change block by block from white to black. This trend continued as blacks moved into West Garfield Park in 1959, and then into Austin in 1963. Some black families were met with violent resistance by whites who were opposed to sharing 'their' neighborhoods with black people. The white residents of these neighborhoods saw what had happened in other Chicago neighborhoods and became fearful that their neighborhood would begin to deteriorate as blacks began to move in. Blockbusting and panic peddling became widespread on the West Side of Chicago. Greedy real estate agents would use the racial fear of white residents to scare them into selling their homes for cheap and then hike up the price and sell to incoming African-American families who had limited options. This process was agonizingly slow as residents saw their neighborhoods changing in slow motion. Block by block, starting in the southeast of Austin and moving northwest, the neighborhood of Austin changed from white to black. Many white residents organized to fight this real estate speculation, not because they wanted to live near blacks, but because it was affecting them just as it was affecting black newcomers. Most whites did not want to move, but when blacks started living on their block, they fled for the suburbs or other white areas of the city. Ultimately, the fear of black people and the profit to be exploited, proved too strong to overcome.

Oak Park had the luxury of timing and resources on its side. Oak Park could learn from Austin's mistakes and had the assets to stop the block by block segregation that occurred just east of Austin Boulevard. In the late 1960's, Oak Park noticed the increase of whites moving out of the blocks just west of Austin Boulevard. Despite the opposition by many Oak Parkers, Oak Park voted 5-2 to enact the fair housing ordinance of 1968, which would be instrumental in preventing the resegregation that was occurring in Austin and throughout the city. The Oak Park Housing Center, now the Oak Park Regional Housing Center, was established in 1972 and fought to counter the block by block racial change that was taking place throughout the West Side of Chicago. Building maintenance was monitored and code violations were enforced in order to prevent deterioration and exploitation of tenants. Oak Park Housing Center fought against blockbusters and panic peddlers. They encouraged whites to stay in Oak Park and carefully allowed integration to occur. Blacks were spaced out in different locations to avoid the block by block changes that were happening elsewhere in the Chicagoland area. Most areas in Oak Park were and continue to be no more than 30% African-American. It took a conscious effort by Oak Park residents and authorities to create the diverse, integrated, and stable neighborhood that Oak Park remains to be today.

#

Do the impacts of the Great Migration and housing discrimination explain all of the inner city problems that exist today? Let's take a look at other factors that led to the different outcomes of two neighborhoods separated by an invisible wall.

America's Peculiar Institution

There was a uniqueness to the American case of slavery. Ten million people, a conservative estimate, were brought to America... hundreds of people were set up in work camps, and hereditary-forced labor was put in place. That's a very different thing than the personal slavery that existed elsewhere. ~ Edward Ball

African slaves were first brought to America on Dutch ships to the Jamestown, Virginia, colony in 1619. Prior to 1619, indentured servants - people who in exchange for their travels being paid for, came to work in the New World (for free) for a designated period of time - provided much needed labor for European settlers. After Bacon's Rebellion, the white planter elite were fearful of rebellion due to the growing anger of poor whites and to some extent, blacks. The white elite made a conscious effort to turn poor whites against blacks.

In her moving book *The New Jim Crow*, Michelle Alexander states, "Deliberately and strategically, the planter class extended special privileges to poor whites in an effort to drive a wedge between them and black slaves. White settlers were allowed greater access to Native American lands, white servants were allowed to police slaves through slave patrols and militias, and barriers were created so that free labor would not be placed in competition with slave labor. These measures effectively eliminated the risk of future alliances between black slaves and poor whites."[24]

European settlers eventually abandoned their reliance on indentured servants and turned to the importation of black slaves. As colonies in the New World expanded in population and land, the demand for free labor grew exponentially and slaves became an extremely lucrative investment.

The process of stealing Africans from their homeland, in various parts of West and Central Africa, became systematic and methodical. Europeans, often with the help of local accomplices, would capture Africans from their homes, put them in shackles, forcibly send them on a grueling journey to one of their predetermined ports, and finally force them onto slave ships that would sail to North America, South America, and the West Indies. This process became known as the Atlantic Slave Trade.

The forced journey was not only terrifying, but often deadly. The unwilling and resistant Africans were then taken aboard the slave ships where they waited for days or weeks until the ships were full of human cargo. The conditions that slaves had to endure aboard slave ships were beyond horrific. They were taken below deck, and chained so closely to other slaves, that they sometimes couldn't roll over without suffocating someone. The air in the slave quarters was hot and stagnant. The smell of human feces and rotting bodies would make many vomit, adding to the already unbearable stench. Because of these abysmal conditions, disease was common both among the slaves and the crew. The insufferable conditions prompted many slaves to commit suicide by jumping overboard to drown. They would also starve themselves to death. The crew adjusted to this practice by force-feeding their human cargo.

It took six to eight weeks to cross the Atlantic and many slaves were unable to endure the inhumane conditions so death rates were high. Authors James and Lois Horton, note in *Slavery and the Making of America*, "Records of this Atlantic slave trade reveal that mortality rates were generally about 15 percent and could range as high as one-third of the slaves during the Middle Passage."[25]

When the slaves, or whatever was left of them, reached their destinations in the New World, their nightmare only continued. They came off the ships half dead and sold at auctions. Slaves were bought based on their value, or in other words how much profit could be sucked out of them by their masters. Slaves were subjected to various forms of humiliation as potential buyers would inspect them as if they were animals.

Families were often ripped apart when they were sold to different slave owners, sometimes in completely different parts of the United States. The impact of losing loved ones was often times harder to cope with than the daily physical abuse and degradation. Although most whites believed that blacks were not capable of having the same emotions as whites, slaves expressed the utter horror of being torn apart from their families in a strange and terrifying new world.

"Many slaveholders answered charges that the trade (internal slave trade) was inhumane by arguing that slaves were limited in their ability to form human attachments and thus were not affected by being separated from other family members,"[26] the Hortons wrote.

Once slaves reached their destination, most slaves were either house slaves or field slaves. Being a house slave was much preferred as it was generally considered less demanding. Slaves aided in the production of crops such as tobacco, rice, sugar, and cotton. As slavery continued to grow in the United States, cotton became the gold of crops. Cotton was the leading export of the United States and eventually produced jobs for many industrial workers of the North. Slavery and cotton became so profitable that the expansion of slavery became essential. The expansion of slavery continued to the south and west as the US government deceived, killed, and forcibly removed Native Americans from their land.

Edward Baptist, author of the fascinating book, *The Half Has Never Been Told*, states:

> In the span of a single lifetime after the 1780s, the South grew from a narrow coastal strip of worn-out plantations to a sub-continental empire. Entrepreneurial enslavers moved more than 1 million enslaved people, by force, from the communities that survivors of the slave trade from Africa had built in the South and in the West to vast territories that were seized also by force from their Native American inhabitants. From 1783 at the end of the American Revolution to 1861, the number of slaves in the United States increased five times over, and all this expansion produced a powerful nation. For white enslavers were able to force enslaved African-American migrants to pick cotton faster and

more efficiently than free people. Their practices rapidly transformed the southern states into the dominant force in the global cotton market, and cotton was the world's most widely traded commodity at the time, as it was the key raw material during the first century of the industrial revolution. The returns from cotton monopoly powered the modernization of the rest of the American economy, and by the time of the Civil War, the United States had become the second nation to undergo large-scale industrialization.[27]

Contrary to other countries that imported the highest percentages of slaves, the United States was able to increase its total number of slaves without importing more by obtaining young women who would birth future slaves.

According to Edmund Morgan in his book *American Slavery, American Freedom*, "American slaves had both higher birth rates and lower mortality rates than those elsewhere in the Americas.... In 1810, the 1.1 million slaves in the United States constituted almost twice the total number it had imported from Africa during the preceding two centuries; during the next fifty years, the slave population more than tripled again, to almost 4 million in 1860."[28]

Slavery was an unstoppable force that needed a civil war to end.

Almost a century before the Civil War was underway, the Americans fought for independence. Many African-Americans, both slave and free, fought in the Revolutionary War. Some took up arms with the rebels and others battled alongside the British. Many blacks fled to British territory during this time to escape the horrors of slavery. The colonies eventually proclaimed victory over the British and declared their independence. But what became the role of African- Americans in this newly declared free country?

Thomas Jefferson wrote in the Declaration of Independence: "We hold these truths to be self-evident, that all men are created equal, that they are endowed by their Creator with certain unalienable rights, that among these are life, liberty and the pursuit of happiness."

However, this powerful proclamation did not apply to blacks, of

31

course, nor women and Native Americans. It would take decades and even centuries for these groups to attain these so-called unalienable rights. In fact, 11 years after the Declaration of Independence was written, black slaves were legally considered to be three-fifths a person, which was more than most whites considered them to be.

Today most people are educated about the atrocities of slavery. Nevertheless, I have still heard people make statements to the effect that slavery wasn't that bad or that there were some good slave owners, or that European immigrants had it just as bad as blacks and overcame their hardships. Many also believe that whites could not enslave Native Americans because they were too stubborn or difficult, implying that African-Americans could be enslaved because they were more submissive and less intelligent. There is also the widespread myth that slavery was not the main cause of the Civil War.

Let's take some time to discuss these misconceptions, starting with the suggestion that slavery was not that bad because there were many good and decent slave owners who fed, housed, and gave their slaves medical attention. Abraham Lincoln dispels this myth in one sentence. He said, "Whenever I hear anyone arguing for slavery, I feel a strong impulse to see it tried on him personally." So unless you are willing to be a slave yourself, you should probably refrain from using this argument.

The notion that there were good slave masters is absurd. It is true that some slave masters treated their slaves better than others, but that does not take away the fact that they still stole someone's freedom. Nobody in their right mind voluntarily deprives themselves of their freedom. People risk their lives for freedom, not because they want to die, but because freedom is essential to every human being. The good slave holders may not have beaten their slaves, but they still viewed themselves as superior to their slaves. I contend that anyone who believes they are superior to another person or another race is not what I would consider a person of good character. Most of these so-called good slave holders would sell their slaves and break up families without thinking twice, if it meant an increase in profit for them.

Then there were the bad slave owners. These people would beat, humiliate, and sometimes kill slaves for the most minute infractions or simply for their own amusement and pleasure.

Morgan writes, "Slaves who transgressed could look forward to a wide range of gruesome punishments—most imposed informally by owners and overseers but some officially meted out upon sentence by special slave courts that existed in all the Southern colonies; including branding; nose slitting; amputation of ears, toes, and fingers (and less often of hands and feet); castration; and burning at the stake."[29]

Regardless of what kind of slave master you were, you were simply that: a slave master. You were someone that deprived another human of their inherent right to freedom. We should not only blame the slaveholders, who had the most obvious impact on slaves, but all of those who made slavery possible and allowed it to persist and even thrive. Edward Baptist illustrates the wide scale horror of this institution:

> The worst thing about slavery as an experience, one is told, was that it denied enslaved African-Americans the liberal rights and liberal subjectivity of modern citizens. It did those things as a matter of course, and as injustice, that denial ranks with the greatest in modern history. But slavery also killed people, in large numbers. From those who survived, it stole everything. Yet the massive and cruel engineering required to rip a million people from their homes, brutally drive them to new, disease-ridden places, and make them live in terror and hunger as they continually built and rebuilt was supposedly focused primarily not on producing profit but on maintaining its status as a quasi-feudal elite, or producing modern ideas about race in order to maintain white unity and elite power.[30]

Another argument is that other minorities and races have been subjected to harsh treatment in America but have overcome and succeeded. It is in fact true that many other minorities have and still are subjected to discrimination and racism, leading to a less than ideal life. There are countless

33

examples of minorities in countries all over the world that have been subjected to inhumane treatment. Immigrants coming from Germany, Ireland, and Italy to name a few were often given inferior jobs, lower pay, or rejected entirely from the workplace. They struggled finding adequate housing and were often the targets of various kinds of abuse.

Yet this harsh treatment hardly compares to the cruel, systemic treatment that black Americans have had to endure since arriving in North America four centuries ago. There was no Irish-American slavery; there were no water fountains separating Germans and whites; and there was no widespread lynching of Italian immigrants. African-Americans were brought over to America against their will and have suffered for centuries at the hands of the very government and people that claim to live in the land of the free. But I guess *free* only refers to those who are determined worthy.

A more widespread misconception is that whites were not able to sustain Native Americans in slavery because they were too resistant, implying blacks did not resist and were somehow indifferent to being slaves. This way of thinking is ignorant of the fact that Native Americans had been living in North America for centuries. They knew the land like no one else. This gave them an extreme advantage when compared to Africans who had been taken from their homeland into a country that was completely unfamiliar to them. They did not have the luxury of developing a life in freedom before their servitude. Blacks entered America weak, hungry, and tired. They were forced off slave ships in chains into a country that was as foreign to them as Africa was to most whites.

Many slaves were entirely unaware that there were people with white skin. When Africans were captured in their homelands, it was usually the first time they had ever seen a white person. Many thought whites were ghosts and were taking them to a foreign place to be eaten.

Howard Zinn, the author of the best-selling *A People's History of the United States*, explains the predicament blacks were in like this: "The Indians were on their own land. The whites were in their own European culture. The blacks had been torn from their land and culture, forced into a situation where the heritage of language, dress, custom, family relations, was bit by bit

34

obliterated except for the remnants that blacks could hold on to by sheer, extraordinary persistence."[31]

This complete unfamiliarity, lack of any resources, and limited opportunities to escape made it almost hopeless to fight back. But fight back they did. Contrary to popular opinion, slaves found many ways to resist their captivity.

Slaves were anything but submissive. Zinn points out that, "From the beginning, the imported black men and women resisted their enslavement. . . Under the most difficult conditions, under pain of mutilation and death, throughout their two hundred years of enslavement in North America, these Afro-Americans continued to rebel." There were only a few organized insurrections. "More often they showed their refusal to submit by running away. Even more often, they engaged in sabotage, slowdowns, and subtle forms of resistance which asserted, if only to themselves and their brothers and sisters, their dignity as human beings."[32]

Perhaps one of the most successful examples of slave resistance happened in 1839 when slaves commandeered the ship *Amistad*. After gaining control of the ship, they attempted to sail back to Africa but were deceived and recaptured. After a long legal fight, they were eventually granted their freedom.

Another example took place in 1841 on the American ship *Creole*, which was sailing out of Virginia to New Orleans with more than one hundred Africans aboard. A group of slaves led by Madison Washington rebelled and managed to take over the ship. The *Creole* ported in the British-controlled Bahamas, where the slaves were temporarily imprisoned. But after black Bahamians threatened to free the slaves by force, the British released them all. These are merely two of more than a hundred instances of revolts aboard slave ships.

Once in America, the resistance continued. Some slaves showed their contempt by sabotage, intentionally performing tasks incorrectly or working slowly. Many slaves would run away, despite knowing the dire consequences that awaited them if captured: whipping and other forms of torture such as amputation of their toes.

The most violent and risky type of resistance was full out rebellion.

Slaves and sometimes free whites and blacks would conspire together. One example of this tactic occurred in 1822. Denmark Vesey, a former slave turned free black man, organized a rebellion in Charleston, South Carolina.

According to *Slavery and the Making of America*, "Their plan was to attack a city arsenal to secure firearms and then to assault the guardhouse, killing as many of the city guards as possible before burning the city and conducting raids in the surrounding countryside. Finally, the rebels would seize ships in Charleston harbor and all would sail for the safety of Haiti." Prior to the date that Vesey set for the uprising to take place, the authorities got word of the plan. "Denmark Vesey and seventy-one other blacks were convicted of plotting insurrection, and thirty-five, including Vesey, were hanged."[33]

Another significant rebellion involved a Virginian slave by the name of Nat Turner. In 1831, Turner and other slaves took up arms and rampaged through Southampton County, Virginia, killing as they went from one plantation to another.

The Hortons describe this event:

> They halted on the outskirts of the county seat, Jerusalem, to recruit more men for an attack on the town, and there a small contingent of white militia confronted Turner's divided forces. During the ensuing fight, Turner and his men routed the militia but then themselves were attacked by white reinforcement from the town. Some men escaped including Turner, but most, including Turner, were eventually found only after they massacred sixty-one whites. Once Turner was captured, he was tried, convicted, and hanged. A huge crowd gathered to witness his hanging, after which surgeons skinned and dissected his body, parceling out portions as souvenirs of the occasion. Decades after his execution, it was possible to purchase purses fashioned from Turner's skin, and trophies made of his bones became southern family heirlooms.[34]

These are only two examples of the more than 250 slave rebellions that have been documented in North America. But unlike Haitian slaves,

American slaves never succeed in overthrowing their white masters. White slave owners knew the power repression had on reducing the hope and power slaves had to end slavery. As each rebellion occurred, white slaveholders became increasingly more paranoid and fearful. So in turn they reacted with acute vengeance to inhibit future revolts.

Laws were also enacted or modified to place more restrictions on the movements and actions of blacks. For instance, following Nat Turner's rebellion, Virginia passed laws that required blacks to get written permission from their owners or overseers to conduct religious services or hold meetings at night. And teaching slaves to read or write was prohibited.[35]

Virginia even considered legislation that would remove all free blacks from the state. Other states prohibited African-Americans from entering at all. Some tried to deport free blacks back to Africa. Free blacks in the North were also at risk of being kidnapped and sent into slavery, as recounted in Solomon Northup's memoir *Twelve Years a Slave*. Other restrictions on voting, carrying firearms, education, and travel made it almost impossible for blacks to successfully gain any leverage on ending slavery.

There were many factors leading to the breakout of the Civil War, but slavery was at the heart of it all. The prominent Civil War historian and Pulitzer Prize-winning author for *Battle Cry of Freedom*, James McPherson describes the causes of the Civil War in three parts.

> First, the issue of slavery and its expansion—which built up over decades and accelerated in the period between 1846 and 1860—came to a head in the presidential election of 1860, causing the deep South states to secede when Abraham Lincoln's election convinced them they had lost control of the national government and, therefore, of slavery's fate within the Union. Second, Lincoln's determination not to compromise on the issue of slavery's expansion. Third, Lincoln's dedication to resupply rather than abandon Fort Sumter, and the decision of Jefferson Davis' administration to fire on federal troops at the South Carolina fort.[36]

Once the slave-owning South was convinced that slavery and its expansion was in serious jeopardy, conflict was imminent. Everything revolved around the South's determination to not only conserve slavery but to expand it. The rest was just adding fuel to the fire.

Today, many people still hold on to the idea that the Civil War was fought over states' rights. This actually, is not so surprising. After the Civil War, history books in the South were written to diminish the horrors of slavery and to distort the truth about the causes of the Civil War.

James W. Loewen, author of the bestselling book *Lies My Teacher Told Me*, explains, "Before the 1960s, publishers had been in thrall to the white South. In the 1920s, Florida and other Southern states passed laws requiring 'Securing a Correct History of the U.S., Including a True and Correct History of the Confederacy.' Textbooks were even required to call the Civil War *the War between the states*, as if no single nation had existed which the South had rent apart."[37]

He argues that students of all ages were brainwashed by distorted facts and half-truths for decades. There are also organizations like the United Daughters of the Confederacy (UDC) that were formed after the Civil War and are still alive and well today. This organization and many alike, have tried to change the perception of why the Civil War was fought in the pursuance of the false reality that the Confederacy was formed for a noble cause. It is much easier to change the past to a more convenient history in order to justify the deaths of thousands. Indeed, it is not pleasant to think that your ancestors died fighting to uphold slavery, but many textbooks that are still used in schools give a watered down history of our racial past. We cannot fully move forward until we confront our past, as ugly and difficult as it may be.

When most people think about the abolition of slavery, Abraham Lincoln comes to mind. To be sure, Lincoln played a major role in ending slavery, but it is inaccurate and misleading to believe that Abraham Lincoln was solely responsible. Throughout history, it is common for politicians to get credit for changes driven by the efforts of citizens. The abolition of slavery in the United States is no exception. Abolitionists like Frederick Douglass, who gave first-hand accounts of slavery's horrors, gained support for ending slavery. William Lloyd Garrison's newspaper, the *Liberator*, broadened the awareness of slavery. Harriet Beecher Stowe's novel, *Uncle Tom's Cabin*, added to the already growing sentiment against slavery. Harriet Tubman, with the help of many fugitive and free blacks, gave hope to the enslaved. It was people like them that started to change the way people thought about slavery.

This growing movement against slavery created by white abolitionists, free blacks, and fugitive slaves struck fear into the slaveholding South, which fought back by doing what they did best: inducing fear and criminalizing dissent. Substantial rewards were offered for the arrests of abolitionists and anyone distributing information supporting and encouraging the abolishment of slavery. As the abolishment movement grew, so did the South's determination to not only keep the Southern way of life, but also to expand slavery.

There is not one underlying cause of the Civil War but many, and all revolved around the issue of slavery. The divide between the North and the South continued to widen as the nineteenth century progressed. There were a couple of key events that amplified the already ignited tensions between the North and the South. Abolitionists in the North were furious as the Fugitive Slave Act of 1850 forced Northern states to return runaway slaves to their rightful owners in the South.

Four years later, the Kansas-Nebraska Act opened the Kansas territory to slavery. This led to a violent conflict known as Bleeding Kansas, which increased tensions. In 1857 Dred Scott sued his deceased master's wife, Eliza Sanford, claiming he was legally free because he had lived with her late husband John Emerson in the Wisconsin Territory, where slavery was illegal. The case made it all the way to the Supreme Court.

Chief Justice Roger B. Taney declared that African-Americans— whether free or slave—were not, and could never become, American citizens and thus had no right to sue in federal court. In 1857 the Supreme Court also ruled that Congress lacked power to ban slavery in US territories and declared that the rights of slave owners were constitutionally protected by the Fifth

Amendment because slaves were legal property.[38]

Two years later a white abolitionist named John Brown, accompanied by more than 20 whites and blacks, seized the federal armory and arsenal at Harpers Ferry, Virginia. His plan was to encourage free blacks to start a rebellion with him to annihilate slavery in Virginia. Ultimately his plan failed when the US Marines, led by Robert E. Lee overtook Brown and his crew.

Brown was captured and later hanged, but not before exclaiming, "I John Brown am now quite certain that the crimes of this guilty, land: will never be purged away; but with blood."[39] His prediction soon became a reality.

After Abraham Lincoln was elected president in 1860, Southern anger reached its peak. Not long after Lincoln won the presidency, South Carolina became the first state to secede from the Union and was soon followed by Mississippi, Florida, Alabama, Georgia, Louisiana, and Texas. Finally, Virginia, Arkansas, Tennessee, and North Carolina seceded to join what became the Confederate States of America. When federal troops led by Major Robert Anderson refused to surrender Fort Sumter, the Confederates attacked, provoking Lincoln to call up troops. The bloody, American Civil War was underway.

Freedom?

The slave went free; stood a brief moment in the sun; then moved back into slavery.
~W.E.B. Dubois

As the fierce fighting of the Civil War was underway, the role of black men and women was debated by both the North and South. It seemed obvious that the North would use all the men they had available to fight in the war; however, the North was hesitant to allow blacks to serve in the Army.

In *Slavery and The Making of America*, the Hortons state, "Most whites, including Lincoln and other government officials, refused to believe that they (African-Americans) would make good soldiers. Whites believed that ex-slaves in particular, by nature and training, were too submissive and cowardly to fight, especially when the enemy was their former masters."[40]

Blacks served and fought in both the American Revolution and the War of 1812 and had proven their worth on the battlefield, but due to white prejudices and racism, they were not embraced as soldiers at the beginning of the Civil War. Frederick Douglass observed the hypocrisy of White America, when he said, "Colored men were good enough... to help win American independence, but they are not good enough to help preserve that independence against treason and rebellion."[41]

Ironically, many soldiers in the North offered to help put down slave rebellions in the South and also returned runaway slaves to their masters. However, as the Civil War progressed the attitude and policies regarding the role blacks played in the Army started to shift.

The change in attitude of many whites in the North was not due to a newfound feeling that blacks were suddenly thought to be their equal. Instead, it had more to do with the strategic fact that the South was more resistant than initially thought. One key event took place at Fortress Monroe, Virginia, when three runaway slaves crossed into Union territory there. But instead of returning the fugitives back to their owners, General Benjamin Butler kept them in Union territory and put them to work.

As word of this event traveled, hundreds of fugitive slaves escaped to Union lines. These ex-slaves became known as contraband. Within a few months there were some nine hundred contrabands under Butler's control.[42]

As a high rate of Union soldiers were losing their lives and as the North was finding it more and more difficult to recruit whites into the Army, a reluctant Lincoln finally agreed to allow blacks to volunteer for service. Former slaves and free black men joined the fight against the Confederate South and their persistent belief in upholding slavery.

African-Americans played a significant role in the eventual Union victory. While their impact was great, so was the adversity they had to overcome as they fought amongst whites. It was determined that blacks would serve in segregated regiments and be commanded primarily by white officers. Not only were blacks not able to lead their own segregated regiments, but they received less pay, and were given inferior food, clothing, jobs, and assignments. Leon F. Litwack's *Been in the Storm So Long* states, "Of the many grievances, the most deeply felt and resented was the inequality in pay, the fact that white privates were paid $13 a month plus a $3.50 clothing allowance, while blacks received $10 a month, out of which $3.00 might be deducted for clothing."[43]

Another problem African-Americans faced was the issue of how they would be handled as prisoners of war. In many cases, it was decided not to take any. Because blacks were not considered citizens, they had no rights and were often murdered after they surrendered. Others were sold back into slavery or put to work for the Confederate Army.

Some ex-slaves actually thought they had been treated better in the South. "The thousands of slaves who flocked to the Union lines were apt to encounter the same prejudices, the same exploitation, the same disparagement, the same capacity for sadistic cruelty which they thought they had left behind them on the plantations and farms. To belittle the slave's character dress, language, name, and demeanor, to make him the butt of their humor, to ridicule his aspirations, to mock his religious worship, to exploit his illiteracy were ways of passing the duller moments of camp."[44]

Despite the constant discrimination against black soldiers, they persisted and were a vital part of the impending Union victory. "By the end of the Civil War, more than 186,000 black men, most of them (134,111) recruited or conscripted in the slave states, had serviced in the Union Army, comprising nearly 10 percent of the total enrollment. Almost as many blacks, men and women, mostly freedmen, were employed as teamsters, carpenters, cooks, nurses, laundresses, stevedores, blacksmiths, coopers, bridge builders, laborers, servants, spies, scouts, and guides.[45]

As discussed earlier, the many negative stereotypes whites and the federal government had of blacks that initially prevented blacks from enlistment in the Army proved to be untrue, and blacks proved to fight as well as whites.

It was a huge concession for white men to admit that black men were their equal, at least in terms of combat. Litwack asserts, "Whether by guarding prisoners, marching through the South as an army of occupation, or engaging Confederate troops in combat, the black soldier represented a sudden, dramatic, and far-reaching reversal of traditional roles."[46]

It is uncertain whether the North would have beat the South without the help of African-Americans, but what is certain is that blacks not only had a critical role in the winning of the Civil War, but they also changed the perception of whites in their ability to fight as well as anyone. Blacks could take pride in their role in helping their fellow man draw that much closer to freedom.

Abraham Lincoln, known as the Great Emancipator, was more of a reluctant emancipator or a politically-minded emancipator. Lincoln did not believe that blacks were equal to whites. In fact, during his fourth debate with Stephen Douglas, Lincoln told an audience in Charleston, "I will say, then, that I am not, nor ever have been, in favor of bringing about in any way the social and political equality of the white and black races; that I am not, nor ever have been, in favor of making voters or jurors of negroes, nor of qualifying them to hold office, nor to intermarry with white people.

"And inasmuch as they cannot so live, while they do remain together

43

there must be the position of superior and inferior, and I as much as any other man am in favor of having the superior position assigned to the white race."

For a while, Lincoln's proposed solution to the negro problem was to ship them back to Africa. But as the abolishment movement gained momentum, Lincoln moved toward the idea of emancipation. However, his first proclamation in 1862 had ulterior motives. It was more a military than social move that gave the South four months to stop rebelling or else he would emancipate their slaves. States that rejoined the union could keep slavery.[47]

Finally, when the Emancipation Proclamation was issued on January 1, 1863, it declared slaves free, but only in areas that were currently fighting the Union. Not only was the Emancipation Proclamation limited, but it was only a pronouncement. Slaveholders were not going to suddenly give up all their slaves because Lincoln declared them free. Nevertheless, it was undoubtedly a step in the right direction.

The senate adopted the Thirteenth Amendment, declaring an end to slavery and eventually the House of Representatives followed suit. As slaves got word of this, many became more willing to take their chances and escape. But just as many stayed with their masters. Most slaves had nowhere to go and their lack of resources made it challenging to just up and leave.

As April 1865 approached, the Confederacy was on its last legs and defeat seemed imminent. When Robert E. Lee surrendered at Appomattox Court House on April 9, 1865, the North had finally won after four long years of fighting and suffering more than 600,000 dead.

Many now former slaves were elated by their new status as free men. But they were in a peculiar situation. First of all, areas in the South not affected by the war did not have to free their slaves. In other areas covered by the Emancipation Proclamation, Litwack notes, "For numerous slaves, freedom came only when *de guvment man* made his rounds of the plantations and forced the planters to acknowledge emancipation. The mere threat of such visits and the rumors that Union soldiers were patrolling the countryside in search of offenders prompted a number of holdouts to free their slaves."[48]

Slaveholders that were isolated enough from Union soldiers refused to set their slaves free and in many cases, kept their slaves ignorant of the fact that they were, indeed, free. Most slaves were resourceful enough to find out about their freedom, but this was difficult in certain situations where their masters kept a close eye on them and disallowed any freedom of movement.

Slaveholders were utterly distraught and furious over emancipation, which they often took out on their slaves. Out of outright fear, many slaves did not run away. Still, every master approached emancipation differently. Some appealed to their slaves' complete powerlessness. To justify the enslavement of human beings, slaveholders, convinced themselves that they were caring, parental figures to their slaves. They believed that the blacks' natural state was slavery. In the minds of most slaveholders, they thought that they were doing their slaves a favor by feeding them, clothing them, and giving them a place to live.

According to Litwack, "As slaveholders, many of them had preferred to view the 'peculiar institution' as an obligation and a burden, binding them to feed, clothe, and protect the blacks in return for their labor and obedience."[49]

It truly never crossed the slaveholders mind that they were behaving immorally. Some even believed that they were doing the work of God by providing African-Americans with the necessities to live.

As slave masters communicated this father-like compassion, many slaves chose to stay. Out of no fault of their own, slaves were dependent on their masters because they had no place to go and no money to their name. Other slaves chose to take their chances and run away, but many returned on their own accord unable to survive on their own.

Litwack illustrates this predicament. "After only a brief flirtation with freedom, some slaves drifted back to the plantations and farms from which they had fled. On a number of places, nearly every slave left at some point during the war, not necessarily together, but most of them returned within several weeks or months. Nor was it uncommon for slaves to return only to leave again. Homesickness, the families they had left behind, and disillusionment with the empty content of their freedom, compounded still further by near starvation and exhaustion, drove many back to the relative

45

security of the plantation."[50]

Slave masters were also dependent on their slaves. They were only able to make a living because of free farm labor. Many families also relied on their slaves to perform skilled labor, cook, clean, and do many other tasks that were vital to the sustenance of Southern life. The mutual dependence slaves and their masters had on each other, made the transition to freedom that much more complex.

After the Confederate defeat, it took months and even years before Union soldiers reached slave plantations. Many times the military had to forcibly remove slaves from their slave masters. But the Union soldiers weren't quite the gracious liberators of slaves as they were perceived to be. Many Northern soldiers were forced to fight. Others fought because they despised the Confederacy. And still others joined the military for the money. When a frustrated slave asked a Union soldier why he was stealing from slaves, when he was supposed to be fighting for the slaves, the soldier replied, "You're a God damn liar. I'm fightin' for $14 a month and the Union."[51]

Some Northerners did believe that slavery was evil and needed to be abolished, but they were far from the idea that blacks were their equals. They came storming through the South with their own prejudices, biases, and racist sentiments. The Union soldiers tore through the South burning and looting plantations affecting slave owners and slaves alike. Slave quarters and their possessions were burned or taken, leaving them with even less.

Litwack observed, "To strip the slave of his dignity and self-respect was not enough. Some Yankees exploited his ignorance and trust to defraud him of what little money or worldly goods he possessed."[52]

Black men, women, and children were all affected by Yankee abuse. Like Southerners, most Yankees believed "the racist notion of black women as naturally promiscuous and dissolute....Whatever the reputation of black women for promiscuity, and sexual submission frequently had to be obtained by force."[53] Rape and sexual assault were not uncommon during Union occupation. Some slaves felt that they were treated so poorly by Union troops that they claimed their masters treated them better than the Yankees.

46

The period after the Civil War (1865 to 1877) is known as Reconstruction, when African-Americans gained more rights and their quality of life benefited with this increase of opportunities. This is not to say that the post-slavery transition was free of obstacles. The lives of blacks were difficult and full of hardships, but it is undeniable that the United States was heading in a direction that was conducive to the increased livelihood of African-Americans.

The Radical Republicans—who fought for the civil rights of blacks—greatly influenced American policy towards blacks. During this time, the 14th amendment, which granted African-Americans citizenship, and the 15th amendment, which gave blacks the right to vote, were monumental in promoting the rights of blacks.

According to History.com: "African-American participation in Southern public life after 1867 would be by far the most radical development of Reconstruction, which was essentially a large-scale experiment in interracial democracy unlike that of any other society following the abolition of slavery. Blacks won election to southern state governments and even to the U.S. Congress during this period. Among the other achievements of Reconstruction were the South's first state-funded public school systems, more equitable taxation legislation, laws against racial discrimination in public transport and accommodations and ambitious economic development programs (including aid to railroads and other enterprises)."[54]

The claim that the more than four million freed slaves were responsible for the post-Civil War chaos is blatantly untrue. Immediately after the Civil War, much of the chaos was the result of Confederate guerrilla warfare against Union troops. Many Confederate soldiers and sympathizers including Jefferson Davis, the president of the Confederacy, refused to surrender without a fight. Douglas Blackmon, in his Pulitzer Prize-winning book, *Slavery by Another Name*, contends, "The increasing lawlessness of the postwar years was, rather than a wave of crime by freed slaves as so often claimed, largely perpetrating against whites by other whites."[55]

Still, the white-on-white violence was only part of the turmoil of post-Civil War southern life. The daily life of the newly freed slave was a struggle. Finding work, locating long lost kin, and obtaining the necessities of life were an indisputable part of their daily grind. Aggravating these dilemmas were the perpetual injustices that ex-slaves had to overcome. The relationship between whites and blacks changed. Prior to the freeing of slaves, it was in the slave holders' best interest to protect their slaves because of the investment they had in them.

Litwack wrote, "With black men and women no longer commanding a market price, the value placed on black life declined precipitately, and the slaves freed by the war found themselves living among a people who suffered the worst possible ignominy, military defeat and 'alien' occupation."[56] One white Southerner summed up this idea by stating, "Niggers life is cheap."

It was not uncommon for a black to be beaten, arrested, or even murdered for not acting in concert to the unwritten white etiquette of the South. Litwack describes the post-Civil War struggle of blacks, commenting that "of the countless cases of post-war violence, in fact, the largest proportion related in some way to that broad and vaguely defined charge of conduct unbecoming black people—that is putting on airs, sassiness, impudence, insolence, disrespect, insubordination, contradicting whites, and violating racial customs. Behavior which many blacks and outside observers deemed relatively inoffensive might be regarded by certain native whites as deserving of a violent censure."[57]

It was expected that a black show the utmost respect for whites at all times. However, this respect whites demanded was a double standard, as whites did not have to show any signs of respect to blacks. It was also a way of exhibiting their superiority over blacks and ensuring that blacks understood their lesser role in society.

Litwack says, "What was permissible behavior for a white person, in other words, was not necessarily permissible behavior for a black man or woman. When freedmen declined to remove or touch their hat upon meeting a white person, or if they failed to stand while they spoke with whites, they were 'growing too saucy for human endurance.' When freedmen took to promenading about the streets or public places, refusing to give up the sidewalks to every white who approached, that was impudence of the rankest sort."[58]

Despite the fact that blacks were now free, they still had to submit themselves to the written and unwritten laws of the white man. The thought of blacks roaming freely through the South was a terrifying notion to most southerners. Since whites could no longer legally enslave black Americans, they had to find a new way to deal with emancipation. One way was segregation, which strictly controlled black's daily activities to the point where freemen were prevented from going places and doing things they might have been able to do and go as slaves.

Segregation would not take full effect until years after the end of Reconstruction, but it presented itself in the early stages of the post-slavery South. Segregation and other policies that discriminated against blacks became known as black codes under President Andrew Johnson. The concept of segregation has now and always been to designate a group of people to an inferior position in society. This was no exception in the South. Leon Litwack illustrates the many black codes that consumed post-Civil War southern life.

> On the city streetcars, blacks were forced to ride on the open platforms or in separate and specially marked cars. On the railroads, blacks were excluded from first-class accommodations and relegated to the smoking compartments or to freight boxcars in which seats or benches had been placed. On the steamboats plying the waterways and coasts, blacks were expected to sleep on the open deck and to eat with the servants, although they paid the same fares as white passengers....If admitted at all to public places, such as theaters and churches, blacks sat in separate and inferior sections, usually rear seats or the balcony. Few if any public inns or restaurants accommodated them, except for those which catered exclusively to blacks.[59]

In the minds of the white South, segregation was central to averting miscegenation. The fictitious belief that blacks were overtly sexual and lustful justified the separation of blacks and whites—especially black men and white women—as an effort to evade a mixing of races. Segregation would become a central issue of the Civil Rights Movement a century later.

The odds of African-Americans receiving anything that resembled justice in the post-slavery South was grim at best, according to Litwack. "Law enforcement agencies and officers, if not co-conspirators in violating the civil rights of ex-slaves, might be expected to protect or ignore the violators....If a white man should be apprehended and tried for offenses committed against freemen, the chances of convicting him were slight so long as whites dominated the juries. And if convicted, the penalties assessed against him were likely to be far less than the gravity of the crime warranted or that would have been imposed upon a black person."[60]

On the other hand, blacks would be arrested essentially for the unforgiving crime of being black. They would also be convicted at higher rates and typically did not have the money to pay for lawyers or were denied legal counsel and bail altogether. Litwack describes Southern justice.

"After their initial experiences with the judicial system, many freedmen found little reason to place any confidence in it. The laws discriminated against them, the courts upheld a double standard of justice, and the police acted as the enforcers. Arrested often for the most trivial offenses (for which whites would rarely be apprehended), blacks found themselves in jail for months without a trial, denied the right to competent counsel (lawyers feared losing their white clients), charged exorbitant legal fees, and sentences as much for their race as for the nature of their crime."[61]

Been in the Storm So Long quotes a black man in Georgia: "A white man may assault a colored gentleman at high noon, pelt him with stones, or maul him with a club, without any provocation at all; and if it has to be decided by rebel justice, the colored man is fined or imprisoned, and the white man is justified in what he and his friends call a narrow escape."[62]

Clearly, there was nothing just about the justice system in the post-Civil War South.

Passage of the 14th and 15th amendments granting blacks citizenship and the right to vote were undoubtedly great progress, but as with everything in the post-slavery South, it did not come easy for blacks. Many southern whites resented that blacks were citizens with the right to vote. These whites went to great lengths to intimidate blacks from voting. African-Americans faced regular harassment when attempting to perform their constitutional rights.

Another tremendous accomplishment during Reconstruction was establishing many schools for blacks. But the resistance of whites who wanted to keep blacks illiterate was a formidable challenge for many blacks trying to get an education. Black teachers were often mobbed or threatened, schoolhouses were frequently set on fire, and black students were regularly assaulted and intimidated even when attending segregated schools.[63]

As Reconstruction came to a close, the fate of black voting rights and schooling deteriorated at alarming rates.

When Democrats gained control of the House of Representatives and white supremacists started reasserting their power and influence in the South, the progressive reforms attained during Reconstruction started to wane and reverse. Philip Dray, the author of *At the Hands of Persons Unknown* states that a main reason for the ultimate failure of Reconstruction was the government's failure to implement economic reform that included redistribution of some land.[64] In 1877, federal troops were removed from the South and newly elected president Rutherford Hayes's Compromise of 1877 gave Democrats complete control of the South.

This marked the end of Reconstruction and the beginning of yet another dark chapter in the history of African-Americans. Their brief moment in the sun was over and their move back into slavery had begun. After the slaves were set free, former slaveholders faced a momentous problem. Their wealth was built on the back of slaves. Without them, who would pick the cotton, plant the crops, cook the meals, and do all of the other essential jobs that slaveholders were so dependent on? Many southerners attempted to hire former slaves or desperate whites to do this work, but they fell short of the productivity provided by slaves.

The antebellum slavery system was effectively and efficiently designed by whites to induce the most work humanly possible out of their slaves. For example, slaves picking cotton had a specific quota they had to reach regarding how much cotton they picked each day. This quota was always increasing and often unrealistic. If slaves did not meet their quota they were usually whipped. The fear of floggings or other forms of torture put enough fear into slaves that the efficiency of their work was astounding. Free blacks and whites working on plantations for money after antebellum slavery had no intention of working with this kind of efficiency. They not only worked slower, but often abandoned their jobs in hope of something better. Former slave owners lost much of their ability to maintain efficiency.

#

In addition to plantation slave labor, in the last decades before the Civil War, slaves were frequently used as industrial labor. According to Blackmon in *Slavery by another Name,* many slaves worked as "skilled masons, miners, blacksmiths, pattern makers, and furnace workers. Slaves also performed the overwhelming majority of the raw labor of such operations, working as fillers who shoveled iron ore, limestone, and coal into the furnaces in carefully monitored sequence; guttermen, who drew off the molten iron as it gathered; tree cutters, who felled millions of trees; and teamsters to drive wagons of ore and coal from the mines and finished iron to railroad heads."[65]

By the start of the Civil War, railroads owned an estimated twenty thousand slaves. These southern industries provided the South with substantial revenue, saving a plethora of money by using free labor.

The thirteenth amendment of the United States Constitution declares that, "Neither slavery nor involuntary servitude, except as a punishment for crime whereof the party shall have been duly convicted, shall exist within the United States, or any place subject to their jurisdiction." The amendment abolished slavery, but not as a punishment for criminals. So blacks were re-enslaved from the Civil War to World War II in the form of convict leasing and peonage. Both white and black convicts were leased to corporations and farmers, but blacks were leased at a much higher rate, which had a devastating impact on the recently freed blacks. Blackmon illustrates what amounted to a new slavery system.

> By the late 1870s, the defining characteristics of the new involuntary servitude were clearly apparent. It would be obsessed with ensuring disparate treatment of blacks, who at all times in the ensuing fifty years would constitute the vast majority of those sold into labor. They were routinely starved and brutalized by corporations, farmers, government officials, and small-town businessmen intent on achieving the most lucrative balance between the productivity of the captive labor and the cost of sustaining them. The consequences for African-Americans were grim. In the first two years that Alabama leased its prisoners, nearly 20 percent of them died. In the following year, mortality rose to 35 percent. In the fourth, nearly 45 percent were killed.[66]

The brutality of this new form of slavery was horrific. Whites working within this system had no real incentive to treat their convict slaves well. "If [convicts] died while in custody, there was no financial penalty to the company leasing them. Another black laborer would always be available from the state or a sheriff," Blackmon explains.[67]

Let's take a look at how this neoslavery system functioned.

Part of the white dominance of the post-Reconstruction South was a punitive law enforcement system. The sheriffs in most southern counties held an extraordinary amount of power. Blackmon points out, "Law enforcement officers, justices of the peace, certain court officials, and any witnesses who testified against a defendant were compensated primarily from specific fees charged to those who voluntarily or involuntarily came into the court system."[68] Therefore, there was a big incentive to make arrests.

53

Blacks were commonly arrested for crimes they did not commit or victimless "crimes." Vagrancy laws enabled law enforcement to arrest anyone who could not prove they were employed. These laws were almost exclusively used on blacks since discrimination prevented a large number of blacks from finding work.

Blackmon notes, "Few would hire a black worker who did not have the express approval of his or her former white employer to change jobs. Off the farms, only the most menial work could be awarded to African-Americans."[69] In essence, vagrancy laws criminalized unemployment as a way to arrest African- Americans.

Other obscure laws that were applied to blacks included prohibitions against walking along train tracks, selling farm products after dark, and speaking loudly in the company of white women. In some states it was possible to spend five years in jail for the theft of one pig, which fittingly became known as the pig laws. Another way law enforcement could arrest blacks was for carrying a concealed weapon.

"In an era when great numbers of Southern men carried side arms, the crime of carrying a concealed weapon—enforced almost solely against black men—would by the turn of the century become one of the most consistent instruments of black incarceration."[70]

Arrest rates would typically rise as the need for manual labor rose. "Everywhere in the South that could produce coal or iron during the war, southern industrialists were being pressured to increase production at existing mines and furnaces, or to seize and reopen idled business.... Most months, the Teals (Sheriff Teal and his brother of Alabama) arrested fewer than twenty men," Blackmon wrote. "Then suddenly dozens of minor offenders were rounded up over a few days' time and charged with vagrancy, alcohol violations, and other minor offenses. Nearly all were quickly sentenced to hard labor and shipped out within ten days to fill a gap in men at the coal mines."[71]

This shows a deliberate system designed to both control and punish blacks while providing a free workforce to the growing economy of the South.

Now that African-Americans could be arrested for practically anything without any interference, law enforcement was relatively free to do what they wanted with them. After the arrest, the accused would usually receive no defense, and quickly be convicted of the given crime by a bogus judge. The convict could then be leased to a corporation such as the Tennessee Coal, Iron & Railroad Co. to serve their sentence or a person—usually a farmer—who would pay the highly inflated fine of the convict's crime in return for his labor.

By the end of Reconstruction in 1877, leasing black prisoners became a common practice in virtually every state in the South except for Virginia. "Nearly all the penal functions of government were turned over to the company's purchasing convicts. In return for what they paid each state, the companies received absolute control of the prisoners. They were ostensibly required to provide their own prisons, clothing, and food, and bore responsibility for keeping the convicts incarcerated. Company guards were empowered to chain prisoners, shoot those attempting to flee, torture any who wouldn't submit, and whip the disobedient - naked or clothed - almost without limit. Over eight decades, almost never were there penalties to any acquirer of these slaves for their mistreatment or deaths."[72]

Any argument that this new system was not a form of slavery can easily be proved wrong after reading a few passages detailing the living conditions in a slave mine. Douglas Blackmon describes the horror of the slave mine where Green Cottenham, a black man leased as a convict, labored and died.

> Long before sunrise each morning, two white men swung open the doors from the entryway at the center of the wooden prison barrack and pushed into the rancid wooden cavern where Green and two hundred other black men, chained to one another, lay wrapped in coarse blankets. Running the fifty-foot length of the room, a continual series of bunk beds dangling on pipes attached to the ceiling were piled with bodies. Where there was no space on a surface, men draped themselves in suspended contortions across canvas

hammocks stretched between the bunks on either side of a narrow aisle down the center. A single potbellied stove, long gone cold, stood at the center of the room.[73]

Blackmon describes the various forms of torture employed regularly at these slave mines. "*Come-a-longs* were steel bracelets snapped onto the wrists and fastened by a chain to a small metal crossbar. Turning the crossbar instantly twisted a man's arms into a knot, forcing him to his knees. In a punishment known simply as the chains, a prisoner was placed in handcuffs attached to the ends of a thirty-inch steel bar, which was then hoisted with a pulley until the man hung clear of the floor and, to be left suspended from 50 minutes to two hours."[74]

Prisoners would also be forced to wear shackles that were too heavy to run with. Or they would wear shackles that were sharpened, which made it not only impossible to run, but difficult to walk normally. Wearing these shackles would commonly lead to infections that if left untreated would result in the amputation of many prisoners' lower extremities. Whippings with a variety of excruciatingly painful objects were frequent.

Blackmon describes another form of torture:

By far the most torturous and widely used punishment was the 'water cure' a medieval cruciation whose many variations rendered the strongest and most defiant of men utterly compliant. In its most moderate form, the water cure was simply forcing a man to stand naked under a shower of cold water until he convulsed with cold. More often, prisoners described being stripped of their clothing and tied to a post or chair. A water line- often a high pressure fire hose- was turned on the naked prisoner, pounding his skin with intense pressure and filling his mouth and nose with torrents of water until he became convinced he was about to drown.[75]

Torture was not the only way prisoners were injured and killed. The nature of the work and harsh living conditions led to many accidents and disease was rampant. Equally terrifying was the likelihood of never escaping the vicious cycle of injustice. Black prisoners would be given longer sentences.

If a prisoner did manage to escape, he was tracked down by bloodhounds and surely tortured when returned. Many prisoners were lost in the system due to intentionally or unintentionally lost paperwork. These prisoners had no one advocating for them and therefore spent long sentences or died in these slave camps. Some blacks were given proper burials, but most were buried in unmarked graves never to be heard from again.

Another popular way for blacks to be punished and for whites to reap the benefits was peonage, also known as debt slavery. After being convicted of a bogus crime, blacks were given an inflated fine. Most blacks could not pay this fine, so they were taken to a farmer who would pay the fine for them on the condition that the convict would work for them. Poor, vulnerable, and often illiterate African-Americans were manipulated into signing a contract that they usually could not read that essentially made them the farmer's indentured servant.

Southern farmers that participated in peonage usually had multiple laborers. They also paid overseers who enforced discipline on their laborers. These peonage farms were eerily similar to the conditions of slave plantations. The prisoners were often kept locked up at night and driven by the whip during the day. Security was heavy so the chance of escape was rare. Like corporations, the farmers often fabricated stories that the prisoners broke their contracts, and therefore had to stay as forced labor for a longer, undetermined amount of time.

One particularly gruesome example of this type of peonage told by Douglas Blackmon is the story of John S. Williams. When two officers inquired about the eleven black forced laborers working on Williams's farm, he became frightened. To avoid any chance of prosecution, he murdered all eleven of his black forced laborers. Perhaps because of the brutality of this particular incident, Williams and an accomplice were tried and convicted. Williams became the only white man in Georgia found guilty of murdering a black man between 1877 and 1966.[76]

Although there were attempts to reform these forms of neoslavery, most failed. Involuntary servitude became less frequent during and after WWII although the practice persisted into the 1950s.

Perhaps the most terrifying abuse that blacks had to suffer post-slavery, was the epidemic of lynching. Philip Dray chronicles the lynching of Black America in his wonderful but disturbing book *At The Hands of Persons Unknown*. Lynching is defined as "to hang or otherwise kill by mob action in punishment of a presumed crime or offense."

Lynching occurred in both the North and South and whites and blacks were both victims, but victims in the South were disproportionately black. The lynching of Black Americans reached its peak in 1892 when 161 documented lynchings took place. The lynching of Black Americans took place all over the South.

According to Philip Dray, "From Tidewater, Virginia, to Alabama's piney woods, from New Orleans French Quarter to the Texas ranchlands, the South has always held considerable topographical, social, and political diversity, and lynching statistics reflect it. The Deep South accounts for most lynchings, with Georgia, Mississippi, and Texas the dominant lynching states, followed closely by Louisiana, Alabama, and Arkansas."[77]

Lynchings kept African-Americans in a constant state of fear. Especially because blacks would be lynched for the most minute infractions and whites handed out this punishment with almost complete impunity.

Although the most sensational and commonly repeated excuse for a lynching was a sexual assault by a black man against a white woman, the instigating reasons were actually wide- ranging. In 1897, with two or three lynchings making news every week and a total of 123 black victims recorded for the year, the causes of the incidents ranged from murder, rape, and assault to wanting a drink of water and sassing a white lady, In a typical four-week period beginning June 14, 1897, Mrs. Jake Cebrose of Plano, Texas, was lynched for "nothing"; four men accused of murder - Solomon Jackson, Lewis Speir, Jesse Thomson, and Camp Reese - were lynched together in Wetumpka, Alabama; an eight-year-old black child identified only as "Parks" was lynched in South Carolina for "nothing"; Charlie Washington burned at the stake for "assault" in Devline, Louisiana; Dan Ogg was put to death in Palestine, Texas, because he was "found in a white family's room"; and Alex Walker of Pleasant Hill, Alabama, had his life extinguished for "being troublesome."[78]

Lynchings were also excruciatingly troublesome for blacks because they were often condoned by whole communities. One can look at old photographs of blacks hanging dead from a tree surrounded by large groups of whites. A particular chilling photo was taken in Fort Lauderdale, Florida, of Rubin Stacy hanging from a tree as a young group of white girls stare at the dead black men. Rubin Stacy was lynched for allegedly threatening and frightening a white woman.

A National Association for the Advancement of Colored People (NAACP) flyer underneath the photo states: "Do not look at the Negro. His earthly problems are ended. Instead, look at the seven WHITE children who gaze at the gruesome spectacle. Is it horror or gloating on the face of the neatly dressed seven-year-old girl on the right? Is the tiny four-year-old girl on the left old enough, one wonders, to comprehend the barbarism her elders have perpetrated."[79]

Law enforcement was either involved or indifferent to the lynching of blacks. It was not uncommon for gangs of white men to break into local jails, extract the accused black from his cell, and lynch him nearby the jail. Gruesome torture and mutilation was commonplace in lynchings of African Americans. Victims would be burned alive, dismembered, shot, and hung. The mob would find sadistic pleasure in taking their time before killing a black. Many Southern whites chose to take the law into their own hand because they felt the justice system would be too slow, and they did not want to take any chance of the accused being found not guilty.

Dray believes some Southern whites preferred lynching as a "systematized reign of terror that was used to maintain the power whites had over blacks, a way to keep blacks fearful and to forestall black progress and miscegenation."[80] When other forms of racism and discrimination were not enough, lynching kept the black man in his place.

#

Many people are aware of civil rights leaders such as Martin Luther King, Jr. and Malcolm X, but are less familiar with names like Ida B. Wells and W.E.B. Dubois. Despite this, their contributions to society in general, and African- Americans in particular, are no less significant.

Ida B. Wells was born a slave in Mississippi a year before the Emancipation Proclamation. She gained her freedom as the Union defeated the Confederacy in the Civil War. But as we have learned, this freedom was very limited, especially to blacks in the South. Wells always had a strong sense of duty to her people, but events in her life propelled her to be one of the most influential civil rights activists.

Millions of blacks heading north during the Great Migration were forced to sit in the Jim Crow cars when in Southern states, but could switch cars when entering into states that allowed integration. It wasn't only that whites and blacks had to segregate when on trains in the South, but that the Jim Crow cars were far inferior to the other cars that whites could ride in. Philip Dray notes, "For a black woman, travel on Southern trains was often humiliating. They could purchase tickets to ride first class— sometimes a separate, first-class ladies car was available—but local laws or railroad regulations might force them to ride in a colored car, which women in particular disdained because it was usually the train's smoking car and tended to attract rough characters of all types."[81]

One day, Ida B. Wells purchased a first-class ticket from Memphis to Nashville, but was forced to move to the Jim Crow car. Blacks had to purchase tickets for the same price as whites, but could not enjoy the same luxuries. This incensed Wells and she sued the railroad. She initially won a settlement for her case, but it was later overturned.

Wells then began writing articles in opposition for the way blacks were treated in the South. She wrote about the injustice of Jim Crow laws and the negative effects of segregated schools, which got her fired from her job as a teacher.

After one of her friends and two of his associates were lynched in Memphis, she became of the most vocal critics of lynching. She became the owner of the *Memphis Free Speech and Headlight*, and then of the *Free Speech* black newspapers. Her intention was to expose the horrors of lynching and to end the cruel practice.

Philip Dray asserts that Wells was "one of the first Americans to understand that lynching was a form of caste oppression and to recognize that it would have to be exposed to be destroyed, she was also one of the first to articulate its graphic horror."[82]

While Wells was out of town, her office was ransacked, and she was warned that if she ever came back, she would be murdered.

Wells continued her campaign in the North. She wrote articles about lynching for the *New York Age* and fought against the banning of African- American exhibitors at the 1893 World's Columbian Exposition in Chicago. She later led protests in Washington DC, demanding lynching reform by then president, William McKinley. Wells spoke out against the discriminatory employment practices for government jobs during the Woodrow Wilson presidency. She is also known as one of the founders of the NAACP. Ida B. Wells fought all her life for equality and died in Chicago, having a future housing project named after her on the South Side.

W.E.B. Dubois was also one of the most influential black activists of our time. Unlike Ida B. Wells, Dubois was born in Massachusetts and grew up in a more privileged environment. He excelled in school and went on to become the first African-American to earn a PhD from Harvard University. After becoming active in the fight for African-American rights, he published studies and articles in which he elegantly critiqued race relationships in the late nineteenth and early twentieth century. He is famous for *The Philadelphia*

Negro: A Social Study and his book *The Souls of Black Folks*.

He became famous for his opposition against Booker T. Washington's Atlanta Compromise. Booker T. Washington, the famous African-American educator and author, thought that blacks should progress through education and entrepreneurship and not directly challenge Jim Crow, which Dubois publicly rebuked. Dubois would go on to co-found the NAACP, which continued the struggle against white supremacy. Along with other anti-lynching crusaders like Ida B. Wells, Dubois vehemently campaigned against vigilante justice that was so common in the United States during most of his lifetime. W.E.B Dubois passed away one day before Martin Luther King's I Have a Dream speech. He died in Africa where he spent much time advocating for the end of European colonialism throughout the continent.

#

W.E.B Dubois once said: "The slave went free; stood for a brief moment in the sun; then moved back again toward slavery," referring to the initial feeling of freedom being replaced by continued oppression. In 1896, the Supreme Court ruling in *Plessy v. Ferguson* found the concept of *separate but equal* constitutional, essentially legalizing segregation.

Naturally, segregation and many other discriminatory laws and practices expanded after *Plessy v. Ferguson*. Blackmon asserts the decision "legitimized the contemptuous attitudes of whites.... It certified that any charade of equal treatment for African-Americans was not just acceptable and practical at the dawn of the twentieth century, but morally and legally legitimate in the highest venue of white society."[83]

Nearly all meaningful government positions were stripped from African- Americans and then replaced by white Democrats with a goal of reestablishing white supremacy in the South. Blackmon adds, "Virtually no blacks served on state juries. No blacks in the South were permitted to hold meaningful state or local political offices. There were virtually no black sheriffs, constables, or police officers. Blacks had been wholly shunted into their own inferior railroad cars, restrooms, restaurants, neighborhoods, and schools."[84]

Poll taxes, land ownership requirements, and literacy tests were additional ways of excluding blacks from voting because blacks were largely illiterate and poor. These restrictions on blacks largely did not apply to whites as they were grandfathered into voting.

Blackmon details the reissued disenfranchisement of blacks.

> After passage of a new state constitution in 1901, Alabama allowed the registration only of voters who could read or write and were regularly employed, or who owned property valued at $400 or more-a measure clearly aimed at complete elimination of blacks from voting. In Mississippi, only those who were able to pay a poll tax of up to $3 and who could, according to voting registrar's personal assessment, read or understand any clause in the US Constitution could register. Louisiana permitted only those who could read and write or owned at least $300 worth of property. However, any person who could vote on January 1, 1867, or his descendants, was allowed to continue voting regardless of reading skills. This literal 'grandfather clause' guaranteed continued voting rights for illiterate and impoverished whites). South Carolina required literacy or property ownership. North Carolina charged a $2 poll tax and required the ability to read. Virginia, after 1904, allowed to vote only those who had paid their annual $1 poll tax in each of the three years prior to an election and who could fill out a registration form without assistance.[85]

By the beginning of the twentieth century, blacks became fully disenfranchised in the South. In addition to voting, all the progress made to educate blacks was turned upside down. In 1892 the way taxes were distributed to schools changed drastically, and the total number of students, white and black, would determine how much funding a county or town received from the state. Because white students so greatly outnumbered blacks, the consequences were disastrous for minority students.

Blackmon reports, "Overnight, white schools came to receive the vast majority of all funds for education. In one predominantly African-American county, the total budget for black teachers' in 1891 was $6,545-in approximate parity with what was being spent per student at white schools in the county.... Forty years later, the total salaries for teachers instructing 8,483 black children in the county had risen negligibly to just over $8,000. The budget for white teachers, with fewer than two thousand pupils, had climbed by a factor of almost 30, to nearly $60,000."[86]

Also, black teachers' salaries and the duration of the school year at black schools were cut significantly. Whites believed that black children should be working in the field, and that school would take time away from their God-given purpose as field hands and servants. Many southern whites were also fearful that an educated black would be more prone to revolt and less likely to be subservient. They could not stand the idea that African-Americans could improve their status because this was a direct threat to their belief that whites should always reign supreme.

Although there were many unwritten codes that applied to blacks in the South prior to the twentieth century, the only official law was segregating passengers aboard trains. But the early 1900s introduced Jim Crow laws that solidified a social system that ensured blacks were treated as second-class citizens. In his influential classic, *The Strange Career of Jim Crow*, Van Woodward articulates the beginning of Jim Crow.

> Street cars had been common in Southern cities since the eighties, but only Georgia had a segregation law applying to them before the end of the century. Then in quick succession North Carolina and Virginia adopted such a law in 1901, Louisiana in 1902, Arkansas, South Carolina, and Tennessee in 1903, Mississippi and Maryland in 1904, Florida in 1905, and Oklahoma in 1907. These laws referred to separation within cars, but a Montgomery city ordinance of 1906 was the first to require a completely separate Jim Crow

street car. During these years the older seaboard states of the South also extended the segregation laws to steamboats.[87]

Even though some of the Jim Crow codes were formalized by state law, many were only enforced by city ordinances or local regulations. Regardless of how Jim Crow policies were enforced, they were efficient in separating blacks and whites. "For up and down the avenues and byways of Southern life appeared with increasing profusion the little signs: 'Whites Only' or 'Colored.' Sometimes the law prescribed their dimensions in inches, and in one case the kind and color of paint. Many appeared without requirement by law - over entrances and exits, at theaters and boarding houses, toilets and water fountains, waiting rooms and ticket windows,"[88] explains Woodward.

If African-Americans were not excluded completely from the workplace, they were segregated within the workplace. In addition, "Thirteen Southern and border states required the separation of patients by races in mental hospitals, and ten states specified segregation of inmates in penal institutions.... Segregation of the races in homes for the aged, the indigent, the orphans, the blind, the deaf, and the dumb was the subject of numerous state laws."[89]

Much time and effort was put into segregating every aspect of life that was attainable. Georgia was the first to push blacks out of public parks. Woodward describes the effort and efficiency of the South to segregate virtually every part of life. "Circuses and tent shows, including side shows, fell under a law adopted by Louisiana in 1914, which required separate entrances, exits, ticket windows, and ticket sellers that would be kept at least twenty-five feet apart. The city of Birmingham applied the principle to 'any room, hall, theatre, picture house, auditorium, yard, court, ball park, or other indoor or outdoor place' and specified that the races be 'distinctly separate... by well defined physical barriers.' North Carolina and Virginia interdicted all fraternal orders or societies that permitted members of both races to address each other as brother."[90]

Different types of residential segregation in cities developed in the early 1900s. Some cities segregated certain territories by law and others enforced segregation by intimidation. "The black ghettos of the Darktown slums in every Southern city were the consequence mainly of the Negro's economic status, his relegation to the lowest rung of the ladder.... Smaller towns sometimes excluded Negro residents completely simply by letting it be known in forceful ways that their presence would not be tolerated."[91]

Some Jim Crow Laws were flat out bizarre. "North Carolina and Florida required that textbooks used by the public-school children of one race be kept separate from those used by the other, and the Florida law specified separation even while the books were in storage," Woodward remarks. He continues, "South Carolina for a time segregated a third caste by establishing separate schools for mulatto as well as for white and Negro children. A New Orleans ordinance segregated white and Negro prostitutes in separate districts."[92]

In 1912 when Woodrow Wilson became president of the United States, he quickly segregated the White House. Dray states, "Soon after his 1912 election, Wilson allowed three of his Southern appointees, Secretary of the Treasury William G. McAdoo, Secretary of the Navy Josephus Daniels, and Postmaster General Albert S. Burleson, to begin segregating federal employees in certain Washington agencies, while also downgrading or eliminating a number of black officeholders who were appointed during the Roosevelt and Taft administrations. Cafeterias in some departments were placed off-limits to blacks, and Jim Crow bathrooms were installed in government buildings."[93]

The walls around blacks were closing in tighter and tighter.

To be clear, despite the atrocious treatment of blacks in the South, the North was far from innocent in their own treatment of blacks. The once-vocal North, that fought against slavery, had fallen eerily silent. Opposition to the Jim Crow system and other Southern atrocities had become weak at best.

In his *Race Orthodoxy in the South*, Thomas P. Bailey asked, "Is not the South being encouraged to treat the negroes as aliens by the growing discrimination against the negro in the North, a discrimination that is social as well as economic? Does not the South perceive that all the fire has gone out of the Northern philanthropic fight for the rights of man? The North has surrendered!"[94]

When the United States entered World War I in 1917, many African-Americans enlisted and fought. Also, many blacks migrated to the North in pursuit of jobs that were created by the war. As black soldiers came back after the war, they hoped that their status would be upgraded. To the contrary, whites became increasingly outraged that African-Americans were taking "their" jobs and parading around in military uniforms.

The violence against blacks after the war was devastating to the optimistic African-American, says Woodward. "Some twenty-five race riots were touched off in American cities during the last six months of 1919.... Mobs took over cities for days at a time, flogging, burning, shooting, and torturing at will. When the Negroes showed a new disposition to fight and defend themselves, violence increased."[95]

Some of these riots occurred in the South, but many took place in the North. Lynchings of Black Americans were not uncommon in the post-war North, even veterans still in uniform. The Ku Klux Klan, which had reemerged in 1915, continued the violence and the enforcement of segregation in both the North and the South. Not until the 1940s did any type of positive change happen for blacks in America. And this change would take time, persistence, and an extraordinary amount of courage and strength to overcome the deeply embedded racism that prevailed in the United States of America.

He Had a Dream

Change does not roll in on the wheels of inevitability, but comes through continuous struggle. And so we must straighten our backs and work for our freedom. A man can't ride you unless your back is bent.... Darkness cannot drive out darkness: only light can do that. Hate cannot drive out hate: only love can do that. ~ Martin Luther King, Jr.

To overcome the deeply rooted racism and discrimination that was evident in the United States, radical change needed to occur, and it came in the form of a revolution carried out by ordinary American citizens that would prove themselves to be extraordinary. This second American Revolution would need a leader that could organize, inspire, and instill hope to a nation of second-class citizens. This revolution became known as the Civil Rights Movement and their valiant leader was a pastor from Georgia named Dr. Martin Luther King, Jr.

After the bombing at Pearl Harbor, the United States involvement in World War II became imminent. President Franklin Delano Roosevelt knew the country would need the help of black Americans to fight as soldiers against the Axis powers. More than one million black soldiers served in the segregated armed forces from 1941–1945 and they had a major impact on both the war and on the United States when they returned home.

After serving honorably and bravely in the war, African-American veterans came back to a country that treated them as second-class citizens. Similar to what happened after World War I, black veterans were discriminated against, beaten, and even killed when they returned home from the war. This was in no way a new experience, but the reaction from blacks was more confrontational and aggressive.

The efforts to organize and demand change gained momentum after the Supreme Court declared state school segregation laws unconstitutional in the landmark 194 *Brown v. Board of Education* ruling, which overturned *Plessy vs.Ferguson*'s separate but equal. This monumental decision paved the way for integration and the start of the Civil Rights Movement. The confidence and optimism amongst blacks and other anti-segregationists was on the rise, but so was the resistance of many states in the South.

Similar to the reluctance of slaveholders to set free their slaves, Southern states were not simply going to allow blacks to integrate into schools just because the Supreme Court said so. Woodward describes how with the exception of a few border states, the increased resistance to integration gained momentum, especially in the Deep South.

> Mississippi came forward in her historic role as leader of reaction in race policy, just as she had in 1875 to overthrow Reconstruction and in 1890 to disfranchise the Negro. The third 'Mississippi Plan' took the form of the Citizens Councils, which were started at Indianola in July 1954, to wage unremitting war in defense of segregation.
>
> In the first three months of 1956 the legislatures of five Southern states - Alabama, Georgia, Mississippi, South Carolina, and Virginia - adopted at least forty-two pro-segregation measures, mainly dealing with schools....
>
> The Louisiana legislature would withhold approval and funds from 'any school violating the segregation provision' of its laws. Georgia made it a 'felony for any school official of the state or any municipal or county schools to spend tax money for public schools in which the races are mixed.'
>
> North Carolina would also deny funds to local authorities who integrated their schools, and Mississippi made it unlawful for the races to attend publicly supported schools together at the high school level or below. Both Mississippi and Louisiana amended their constitution to provide that to promote public health and morals their schools be operated separately for white and Negro children.

The school year 1956-57 opened in the seventeen Southern and border states with 723 school districts and school units desegregated, a gain of 186 over the previous year. of those districts that had any Negro pupils, some 3,000 remained segregated.[96]

The resistance against integration of schools in the Deep South remained strong so it was inevitable that these two opposing forces would collide and spark unrest. The first incident of violence over school desegregation occurred in February 1956 when the Supreme Court ordered the University of Alabama to admit its first black student, Autherine Lucy. After mobs threatened Lucy while she was attending classes, the university trustees suspended her, stating it was for her safety and the safety of the students and faculty members. A federal district judge ordered the university to reinstate Lucy. Instead the trustees permanently expelled, claiming she had made "outrageous charges" against them.

Perhaps the most famous event of the desegregation battle happened in September, 1957. Governor Orval Faubus ordered National Guardsmen to prevent nine black students from entering the all-white Central High School in Little Rock, Arkansas. After the students were forced to be removed by a belligerent, angry crowd of whites, President Dwight Eisenhower, who hardly even acknowledged the growing civil rights crisis, sent US soldiers to ensure the students were allowed to reenter the school.

The atmosphere at Central High School was so volatile that federal troops had to stay with the black children the entire year, following them everywhere they went to assure their safety. Despite having personal bodyguards, they were still harassed and bullied the entire year. After the school year was over, Governor Faubus closed the school for the next year. Even though the Supreme Court refused to postpone the integration of all public schools, the resistance of Southern states was proving to be an extremely difficult obstacle to overcome. Woodward notes, "Desegregation of public schools in the South came virtually to a halt. In the first three years after the

Brown decision, 712 school districts were desegregated, but in the last three years of the Eisenhower Administration the number fell to 13 in 1958, 19 in 1959, and 17 in 1960."[97]

In the 1960s there was some improvement. Houston, Raleigh, Knoxville, and Richmond were able to desegregate with little disturbance, followed by Atlanta, Dallas, Memphis, and Tampa. New Orleans would eventually desegregate schools but only after whites boycotted schools and took to the streets. But Alabama, Mississippi, and South Carolina still had not integrated any schools. Despite some progress, nine years after the Supreme Court had called for deliberate speed, fewer than 13,000 black public school students were in school with nearly three million Southern whites.[98]

When James Meredith attempted to register as a student at the University of Mississippi in Oxford all hell broke loose. First, Governor Ross Barnett blocked Meredith's entry into the university. Then federal marshals escorted Meredith in. Locals responded by rioting.

Van Woodward argues, "This was not an attack on Negroes or demonstrators. It was an insurrectionary assault on officers and soldiers of the United States Government and the most serious challenge to the Union since the Civil War. The mob fought with stones, bricks, clubs, bottles, iron bars, gasoline bombs, and firearms... The battle raged all night, and by dawn, when the troops routed the mob, two people had been killed and 375 injured, 166 of them marshals, 29 by gunshot wounds."[99]

Despite the strong resistance, James Meredith was eventually registered. This, however, would not be the last violent incident of his life. Meredith and many others continued the long, hard fight for the integration of schools. Successful desegregation of all public schools would not be implemented for another decade.

As the fight for the desegregation of schools went on, so did the battle against segregated buses, restaurants, housing, and many other areas of Southern life. Activists including students, pastors, teachers, lawyers, blacks, whites, and everything in between started organizing. Dr. King founded the Southern Christian Leadership Conference (SCLC). Other influential organizations fighting against white supremacy and advocating for racial equality during this time included the Student Nonviolent Coordinating Committee (SNCC) and the Congress of Racial Equality (CORE).

Martin Luther King, Jr. and his SCLC were committed to the philosophy of nonviolence. King preached to segregationists, exclaiming, "We will soon wear you down by our capacity to suffer....in winning our freedom we will so appeal to your heart and conscience that we will win you in the process."

Activists fighting white supremacy would be taught how to effectively protest using King's nonviolent approach. These selfless, courageous activists, along with their leaders, would influence public opinion, change racist policies and laws, and ultimately impact the country in ways that could hardly have been dreamed of prior to the start of the Civil Rights Movement.

Few cities were devoted to segregation more than Montgomery, Alabama, the state's capital where slavery flourished for decades and home to the heart of the domestic slave trade. Segregated busing was the status quo in Montgomery and many other Southern cities for decades. Black passengers would be expected to pay their fare at the front of the bus, then exit the bus, and finally reenter through the back of the bus. They would then be required to sit in the back of the bus and give up their seats to whites, upon request. This policy was enforced by law enforcement and other means of intimidation.

On December 1, 1955, a seamstress named Rosa Parks—who not-so-coincidentally was secretary of the Montgomery branch of the NAACP— refused to give up her seat to a white person while riding a bus in Montgomery. Parks was not the first to do this, but her name has become synonymous with the Civil Rights era and the fight against segregation. Rosa Parks described the embarrassment and shame that blacks suffered from due to these unjust policies, when she explained, "Having to take a certain section (on a bus) because of your race was humiliating, but having to stand up because a particular driver wanted to keep a white person from having to stand was, to my mind most inhumane."[100]

Resistance to segregated public transportation was not new to Montgomery. Blacks had successfully boycotted streetcar lines from 1900 to 1902, but segregated seating returned soon after through city ordinances. But Rosa Parks' arrest after refusing to give up her bus seat in 1955 initiated an organized boycott of Montgomery buses, fueled through word of mouth and flyers. The discipline and persistence of the boycotters was truly remarkable. Boycotters either walked or used a carpool system to get them from place to place. At least 75 percent of Montgomery bus riders were African-American so the economic impact was significant. By February 1956, downtown merchants reported losses of more than $1 million. The bus company estimated it had lost 65 percent of its income.

Despite this loss in revenue, Montgomery's city officials stubbornly resisted demands for integration. The boycott lasted for more than one year and ended when a federal court ruled that any law requiring racially segregated seating on buses violated the Fourteenth Amendment to the Constitution.

This was possibly the first, most substantial victory for Martin Luther King, Jr. and the nonviolent protest movement that he championed. In spite of the joy many felt in this victory, attacks on blacks and integrationists became commonplace. Snipers shot at buses, black churches were bombed, and any integrationist could be subjected to violence.

The Civil Rights Era was just beginning and civil rights activists would have much to celebrate and mourn in the years to come. When four black students sat at a segregated Woolworth department store lunch counter in Greensboro, North Carolina, few knew the spark that this would ignite. Sit-ins had been going on for years, but the national publicity that these students aroused provided the fuel to help this movement grow.

Activists received training in nonviolent civil disobedience. The SNCC, which formed shortly after the Greensboro sit-ins, helped recruit, organize, and train large numbers of activists—both black and white—to perform nonviolent protests in many states. Some would enter segregated facilities and request service, which would be denied. When the protesters refused to leave, they would be arrested and carted off to jail while getting national exposure.

The opposition to sit-ins was great. As activists were quietly sitting at counters of segregated restaurants and other facilities, gangs of whites would harass them. The protesters would be called niggers or nigger lovers, have food shoved in their faces and drinks poured on their heads, and were often beaten. The students involved in the sit-ins remained nonviolent as they endured this abuse. They would courageously sit stoically at whites-only counters and showed the discipline to not react in these hostile situations. When police arrived the protesters would not resist, but would still often be beaten and insulted by the police before taken to jail. Due to these brave students and their companions, blacks were slowly allowed to integrate into many public facilities.

Shortly after the campaign for sit-ins evolved, another form of protest emerged. The South did not comply to most Supreme Court rulings involving desegregation and race. In addition to the buses, waiting rooms and terminal restaurants were also segregated. Two groups, the Fellowship of Reconciliation (FOR) and CORE began to challenge the lack of enforcement of the Supreme Court's decision to ban segregated interstate buses through what became known as Freedom Rides. Interracial groups would board buses in Washington DC— blacks sitting in the front and whites in the back—and then travel through the South. They would exit the bus in a predetermined Southern city and then blacks would go into the white waiting rooms, and whites would enter the black waiting rooms. The Freedom Riders would then be arrested and taken to jail.

As Freedom Rides continued, outraged Southern whites began terrorizing riders through violence and intimidation. Taylor Branch, author of *The King Years*, states, "On Sunday, May 14, 1961, a white mob attacked and burned one bus of Freedom Riders outside Anniston, Alabama. Minutes later, a Ku Klux Klan posse severely beat the second busload on arrival at the Trailways station in Birmingham."[101]

Other attacks on Freedom Riders occurred in Birmingham and in Montgomery. US Attorney General Robert Kennedy initially failed to protect the Freedom Riders from the Ku Klux Klan and other white mobs, but he eventually petitioned the Interstate Commerce Commission (ICC) for regulations banning segregation in interstate travel. The ICC issued those regulations in September. Progress was being made at the hands of the fearless and dedicated civil rights workers, but Mississippi and Alabama would continue to prove to be two of the most resistant and hostile states.

Few cities were more segregated in 1963 than Birmingham, Alabama, home to some of the most gruesome labor camps used for convict leasing. Birmingham was often called the Johannesburg of America, referring to its similarities with South Africa's apartheid, or Bombingham because of all the bombings that took place in the city.

In their book *Voices of Freedom*, Henry Hampton and Steve Fayer say, "Since the end of World War II, as many as fifty bombings had rocked the city. Many black churches had been targets, and two synagogues. One black section of town was attacked so often people called it Dynamite Hill."[102]

The Ku Klux Klan was strong in Birmingham, having sympathizers in the police department and local government. Fred Shuttlesworth was a black activist and minister who fought against segregation in Birmingham. He called Birmingham a three-tiered society. "If the Klan didn't stop you, the police would stop you. And if the police didn't, the courts would."[103] Leading the charge against integration in Alabama was Governor George Wallace. In his 1963 inaugural address, he is known for infamously declaring, "I draw the line in the dust and toss the gauntlet before the feet of tyranny, and I say segregation now, segregation tomorrow, segregation forever."

Another formidable enemy of the Civil Rights campaign in Birmingham was Eugene "Bull" Connor, the commissioner of public safety and a renowned racist and segregationist. After he was named commissioner, Connor undercut the police department's civil service policies and used officers as his "personal militia."[104]

Birmingham was so tightly under his iron fist, that it made the town a difficult but strategic place to stage a civil rights battle. Many activists believed that if they could end segregation in Birmingham, then they could end segregation everywhere. Connor and Wallace, with the support of white Birmingham, would battle against Martin Luther King and his nonviolent army, which would turn out to be a climactic point in the struggle for civil rights.

The campaign in Birmingham attempted to open America's eyes to racial injustices. Through this exposure, the movement hoped to put pressure on President John F. Kennedy and the federal government to put a damper on the legacy of racism and segregation. King and his followers would conduct sit ins, boycotts, marches, and other nonviolent protests aimed at breaking the fierce grip of discriminatory policies practiced in Birmingham and elsewhere.

In response to the ensuing campaign, Connor ordered all city parks, playgrounds, and golf courses closed rather than abide by a court order opening them to all citizens. As nonviolent protesters took to the streets, Connor arrested them en masse. After King and others were arrested for conducting a Good Friday kneel-in, the protests and demonstration grew larger by the day. Local jails were filled with protesters, hundreds of them school children. (Despite the criticism over King and his associates of letting children protest, their effect on the movement was undeniable).

As people of all ages marched down the streets of Birmingham, Connor's initial nonviolent approach to the protesters, took a dramatic turn. "As children marched out of Sixteenth Street Baptist Church, Bull Connor arrested more than six hundred, ranging in age from six to eighteen. The next day, as another thousand children gathered at the church, an angry Connor called out the police canine unit and ordered his firemen to rig high-pressure hoses. At one hundred pounds of pressure per square inch, the fire hoses were powerful enough to rip the bark off trees."[105]

Pictures of black girls and boys getting mauled by canines and blasted with fire hoses were as shocking as they were horrific. Crowds started to gather and fight back against the police, resulting in more arrests and more protesters fire-hosed. After days of confrontation, a truce was declared so that negotiations could continue between the movement and the white merchants. The goal of the movement negotiators was to desegregate downtown stores, have black sales clerks hired, and ultimately the desegregation of the city's daily life. On May 10, a desegregation settlement was announced and thousands of demonstrators were released from jail.

A day later, terror struck again in Birmingham when bombs went off at the home of King's brother, A.D. King, and at the SCLC headquarters. The explosions--which came immediately after the Ku Klux Klan denounced Birmingham's business community for negotiating with blacks—led to a confrontation between police and protesters.

According to *Voices of Freedom*, "Troopers, ordered to disperse crowds gathering at the motel, were breaking heads as they moved in, and a full-scale riot ensued as blacks began to fight back. By morning, forty people had been injured, and seven stores set afire."[106]

A few months later, tragedy of the most heinous kind struck again at the Sixteenth Street Baptist Church in Birmingham. At 10:19 a.m. on September 15, 1963, fifteen sticks of dynamite blew up inside the church basement killing four black girls and injuring many more. The church had been a rallying place for the Birmingham Campaign, so it was targeted by members the Ku Klux Klan. After the bombing, people filled the streets and police dispersed them by firing over their heads. A sixteen-year-old boy was killed after being shot in the back by a policeman and a thirteen-year-old boy was shot and killed while riding his bicycle. Although it was practically common knowledge who committed the bombing, no arrests were made until more than a decade after the incident.

Just prior to the Sixteenth Street church bombing, civil rights activist Medgar Evers was assassinated in Jackson, Mississippi, by a white supremacist who was later freed after two mistrials. (He was finally convicted of the assassination of Evers in 1994). These events led to the many more whites and blacks joining the cause. In the decade following the church bombing, close to eight thousand civil rights demonstrations took place across the United States, according to data from the Justice Department. The most notable was the demonstration of more than 200,000 in Washington, DC, where Martin Luther King, Jr. gave his legendary I Have a Dream speech.

Not long after the assassination of Evers, activists launched the fight for voting rights in Mississippi, known as the Freedom Summer. Because of Mississippi's long history of discriminatory practices towards the rights of blacks to vote, less than 7 percent of the state's eligible black voters were registered to vote in 1962.[107]

Many white liberals came from the North to help fight for African-American voting rights with black activist leaders like Fannie Lou Hamer and Bob Moses. Three of these activists, two white and one black, were sent to investigate a church burning in Mississippi. They never came back. The disappearance of these three voting rights activists received considerable media attention and an investigation was opened. A month later their bodies were discovered in shallow graves. The State of Mississippi refused to prosecute the perpetrators, so the federal government had to intervene, but the white supremacists convicted of the gruesome crimes were only given minor sentences.

Freedom Summer managed to register some black voters and brought a degree of national attention to Mississippi, but it was largely considered a failure because of the limited results. An even stronger battle would be needed to win the voting rights of black Americans.

In 1964, Lyndon B. Johnson signed into law the landmark Civil Rights Act that outlawed discrimination based on race, color, religion, sex, and national origin. This new law gave the Civil Rights Movement and the people involved some much needed momentum and optimism. But while African-Americans were beginning to see some level of progress as 1965 rolled in, it was slow and not nearly adequate. Blacks and some whites were sacrificing their jobs, health, and even their lives for the cause of racial justice and equality.

The next fight would start in Selma, Alabama. As activists were organizing and fighting for voting rights in Mississippi, they were doing the same in Selma. Blacks had virtually been disenfranchised since Reconstruction, well over fifty years previous. The requirements of literacy tests and poll taxes were created and enacted to assure that blacks would not be able to vote, and therefore whites could continue to reign supreme in the South. The right to vote was as important an issue as any for the Civil Rights Movement. White segregationists could deal with the consequences of integrating a couple lunch counters or buses, but giving blacks the right to vote would threaten the dominant and oppressive power they held in the South.

SNCC and other activists had been fighting for black enfranchisement in Selma since 1963, but local activists became dissatisfied with the progress being made and invited Martin Luther King and SCLC to join the battle in Selma. Many activists including school teachers and school children were arrested, beaten, and even murdered as they attempted to protest.

Governor George Wallace's racist policies, white segregationists, Klansmen, and Jim Clark, the racist sheriff of Dallas County, Alabama, were responsible for much of the violence and repression of the civil rights workers. During one particular peaceful march to a jail, police turned violent against protestors. When Jimmie Lee Jackson tried to help his parents who were being beaten, he was shot by a police officer and died eight days later.

The Jimmie Lee Jackson murder added fuel to the already raging fire that was blazing through the South and Selma. The SCLC began organizing a march from Selma to Montgomery, more than fifty miles. The goal was to attract national attention to the fight for voting rights. Although there was tension between the SNCC and SCLC, the march began on March 7, 1965, remembered as Bloody Sunday. As the nonviolent army of six hundred protesters approached Edmund Pettus Bridge—named after Edmund Pettus, a Civil War general and leader of the KKK—the protesters were ordered to stop and turn around. Not long after, Alabama state troopers—armed with tear gas, whips, cattle prods, and nightsticks—charged at the peaceful protesters and began violently assaulting the activists.

Luckily, no one was killed, but many were seriously wounded and hospitalized. Others were left with the terrifying memory of state troopers assaulting old men, women, and children. The assault was captured by the media and broadcast on ABC.

The national coverage of Bloody Sunday attracted many new volunteers who were outraged over the images of beaten and bloodied protesters and willing to fight for equality. On March 9, just two days after Bloody Sunday, King led a second march. As King and his nonviolent army approached Edmund Pettus Bridge, the state troopers allowed them to pass. As King saw the state troopers part like the Red Sea, he turned his army around and went back to the church. Many activists and civil rights sympathizers were upset with this move, but King and his associates explained that they did not intend to violate a federal court order to continue the march. Later that night a group of civil rights activists were confronted by a small mob of segregationists. The activists were beaten and James Reeb, a white minister, later died from his injuries.

Governor Wallace made it clear that he had no intention of providing safety to the marchers, so the federal government stepped up by calling in the Army and the Alabama National Guard to protect the marchers as they attempted a third and final march. Two thousand people marched from Selma to Montgomery, and then almost 50,000 supporters met the marchers in Montgomery, where King and other speakers addressed the massive crowd at the state capitol building. In spite of the euphoric feelings of victory, Viola Liuzzo, an Italian activist and mother from Detroit, was murdered by Ku Klux Klan members as she was driving marchers back to Selma. She was one of the many selfless heroes that fell victim to hate and racism.

Not long after this historic march, Congress passed the Voting Rights Act that banned literacy tests, modified poll taxes, and mandated federal oversight of voter registration. This was not enough for James Meredith, the man who had integrated Ole Miss a few years earlier. In June 1966, Meredith announced that he would march from Memphis, Tennessee, to Jackson, Mississippi. The March against Fear, a mere 220-mile hike, was intended to encourage blacks in Mississippi to register and vote. Tragedy struck as a white male shot Meredith twice with his shotgun. Meredith survived, but it was clear that there was still work to be done.

The dynamics of the Civil Rights Movement, which had been raging for over a decade since the Brown decision, were changing. At this point in the civil rights battle, there were many different leaders and organizations that had different ideas and goals. Much of the movement up to this point had been focused on Dr. King's nonviolent direct action approach, which had proven to be effective. But many blacks were growing tired and impatient.

A Muslim convert and minister who became known as Malcolm X was one of the most influential and controversial African-American activists during this time. A powerful public speaker like King, Malcolm X advocated a more radical approach. He believed that King's nonviolent approach would not obtain the results that would free blacks from the oppression of white racists. Malcolm X promoted black supremacy and did not believe in integration. His advocacy for self-defense and the right to use violence as a means of black liberation was contrary to everything Martin Luther King preached.

Malcolm X once stated, "Be peaceful, be courteous, obey the law, respect everyone; but if someone puts his hand on you, send him to the cemetery."

The differences in views between King and Malcolm created tension in the movement and many people started to follow Malcolm X and the Nation of Islam. SNCC and its leader Stokely Carmichael started moving away from its nonviolent roots and started to align itself with Malcolm X's idea of black power. Carmichael eventually joined the Black Panther Party, which was founded by Huey Newton in 1966, for the purpose of monitoring the police in Oakland, California.

Black Panthers exercised their right to bear arms and set up patrols to monitor and hopefully curb police brutality. Although the Black Panthers are mostly remembered as a violent and militant group, which they were at times, they also set up free breakfast programs for at-risk youth, community health clinics, and other social organizations that benefited communities. The Black Panthers would expand greatly over the next decade, but would eventually decline and diminish as the FBI aggressively pursued them by tapping their phones and establishing a public relations effort to discredit and damage them.

King held on strongly to his unflinching resolve to fight black oppression with nonviolence. But he took a turn down a path many thought unwise. As the United States' involvement in the Vietnam War continued to escalate, so did the public's disapproval against it. The SNCC took a public stance against the war and soon after King followed suit. The SCLC and many of King's closest allies thought that a negative public stance against the war would isolate the SCLC from the federal government and take the focus away from the black struggle. However, King could not morally continue the fight for black lives by ignoring the injustices that were occurring in Southeast Asia.

In his famous speech at Riverside Church, King said, "I have worked too long now and too hard to get rid of segregation in public accommodations to turn back to the point of segregating my moral concern. Justice is indivisible. Injustice anywhere is a threat to justice everywhere. And wherever I see injustice, I'm going to take a stand against it whether it's in Mississippi or in Vietnam."

Dr. King was not the only famous dissident of the Vietnam War. Boxing legend Muhammad Ali refused to be inducted into the Army. As a result his heavyweight title was revoked, and he faced possible jail time. Many blacks both morally objected to fighting in the war and also rejected fighting for a country that did not give them full rights.

As Martin Luther King continued to fight to end the Vietnam War, he and the SCLC began what they called the Poor People's Campaign, because despite the significant improvement in the rights of African-Americans, the state that most blacks were still living in was an issue that needed to be addressed. The goal was to bring economic justice to everyone living in poverty. Members of the campaign created a demand list and presented it to congress.

During this time, activists supporting the Poor People's Campaign created a gigantic tent city on the Washington Mall and resided there for six weeks. As the Poor People's Campaign continued on, Dr. King went to Memphis to support sanitation workers. He would not leave alive. On April 4, 1968, King was assassinated by a white racist named James Earl Ray on the balcony of the hotel where he was staying.

When we think about the Civil Rights Movement, Rosa Parks, Malcolm X, or Martin Luther King usually come to mind. This is certainly not a bad thing, given what these extraordinary people accomplished. But what we may overlook is the utter terror that blacks faced during that time. In addition to remembering the sacrifices and victories of civil rights heroes, we should also never forget the violence and repression that blacks faced. We should not overlook the detrimental effects the abuse had on blacks during the 1950s and 1960s and for generations to come. The bombings, beatings, jailing, lynching, assassinations, and other forms of terrorizing cannot and should not be romanticized or forgotten.

We cannot simply say it was just a few bad apples because we need to realize that the oppression of blacks was systemic. It wasn't only politicians like George Wallace who were to blame, but also the politicians that had the power to do something and instead chose silence. It was not only the racist goons that beat, bombed, and murdered blacks who were responsible but the average citizen that decided that it was not their problem and chose indifference. And it certainly was not only the South that discriminated and oppressed blacks because the North was guilty too. And there is no better place to start, then sweet home Chicago.

The Windy City

I have never seen such hostility and hatred anywhere in my life, even in
Selma. The people from Mississippi ought to come to Chicago to learn how to
hate. ~ Martin Luther King, Jr

I would say that I have a love-hate relationship with Chicago. I love
Chicago summers, but I hate Chicago winters. I love the Chicago White Sox
and hate the Chicago Cubs, and I both love and hate the Chicago Bears
depending on which Jay Cutler shows up on Sundays. I most definitely love
Chicago-style hot dogs and deep dish pizza. I adore Millennium Park, Maggie
Daley Park, the Riverwalk, the skyline, State Street, Lake Michigan, and all
that downtown Chicago has to offer. However, I do not like all of the crime,
inequality, segregation, and corruption that seems unending.

It is almost as if there were two Chicago's: one in which people can
walk in the streets without the fear of getting shot, another in which you have
to adapt every part of your being to ensure your safety. One world where you
can take your kids to the park without a worry in the world. The other where
you have to pass or avoid certain streets or corners on your way to the park—
that is, if there's a park that's close and safe enough for you to bring your kids.

One Chicago where you can send your kids to a thriving school, where
things like safety and gangs are an abstract thought. Another Chicago where
you will pass safe passage workers on your way to school, and once you get to
school, you will then have to go through metal detectors surrounded by police
or security guards.

One city that is occupied by upscale restaurants, multi-million dollar
condos and houses, and plenty of nightlife to keep you entertained. The other
city that is occupied by the police and controlled by gangs. One place where
you call the police for protection, and the other where you view the police with
skepticism and fear.

One area where you can dream of going to college and obtaining a successful and lucrative job. And another area in where your future will most likely consist of jail or death. One part of the city that is white, another that is black, and the other third that is Hispanic. This can be seen clearly if you take the Red Line from start to finish. Chicago is a city that is so divided by wealth, color, and race that you would think you were driving into different countries as you pass from one invisible line to another.

Yet, I am proud to be a Chicagoan. I was born in Chicago, and I anticipate that I will also die here. But I am one of the lucky ones. I am privileged enough to live in an area where I don't have to constantly worry about my safety. I have the advantage of living in a neighborhood that is not plagued with violence and poverty. I have the benefit of living in an area where there are jobs. My kids will be fortunate enough to attend schools where they can focus on their education and not have to constantly worry about their safety.

I also have the privilege of being white.

This gives me opportunities and securities that I do not often even realize. I love how Johann Hari articulates white privilege as it relates to the war on drugs in his book *Chasing the Scream*. "I am conscious—now more than ever—that this is a privilege I get because I am white, and middle class, and I live in a corner of Western Europe where the worst of the drug war is not fired into the faces of people like me. I keep thinking of all the people I have met who didn't get this privilege, because of the color of their skin, or because they were born in the wrong place. It isn't right. It shouldn't be this way—and it doesn't have to be."[108]

I'm not saying that I or other people did not have to work hard for the privileges that I have, but I am not ignorant of the fact that I had many opportunities that others are deprived of.

#

Racism in the North was different than racism in the South. People in the North were most likely just as racist as Southerners, it was just not as obvious. There were no signs in the North that declared where blacks could and could not go. Politicians in the North were not as openly and overtly racist, which was more abstract in the North. But it was there, and it was powerful. As Isabel Wilkerson describes:

> Blacks in the North could already vote and sit at a lunch counter or anywhere they wanted on an elevated train. Yet they were hemmed in and isolated into two overcrowded sections of the city-the South Side and the West Side-restricted in the jobs they could hold and the mortgages they could get, their children attending segregated and inferior schools, not by edict as in the South but by circumstance in the North, with the results pretty much the same. The unequal living conditions produced the expected unequal results: blacks working long hours for overpriced flats, their children left unsupervised and open to gangs, the resulting rise in crime and drugs, with few people able to get out of the problems so complex as to make it impossible to identify a single cause or solution.[109]

Blacks in Chicago felt the power of racism as most faced regular discrimination. But not until Martin Luther King came to the city in 1966 did the whole country realize how deeply embedded racism was in Chicago.

Martin Luther King came at a time when Chicago had a reputation of being the Birmingham of the North, which was in no way a compliment. Chicago was considered the most segregated city in the North, mostly because of widespread discrimination in housing. This in part led to the ghastly conditions that many African-Americans lived in. Dorothy Tillman, a member of the SCLC, once commented that blacks in Chicago were worse off than those living on plantations in the south.

Chicago's West Side was thought by many to be even worse than the South Side of the city. In *Family Properties*, author Beryl Satter describes the challenges faced by blacks in Chicago's ghettos:

> Between 10 and 25 percent of the adult population was unemployed. For young people, the statistics were far

86

worse: 25 to 50 percent were unable to find jobs. Those who were employed received very low wages. While the median family income for Chicago as a whole was $6,738 per annum, Lawndale's median family income was $4,981, and almost 25 percent of the area's inhabitants earned under $3,000 a year. Over 31 percent were on some form of public aid, giving the neighborhood the largest concentration of people on welfare of any part of the city... The public schools were abysmal, with many young adults barely able to read at a sixth-grade level ... The high schools were jammed at up to 50 percent overcapacity, and dropout rates reached 60 percent."[110]

The poverty in these neighborhoods was devastating. Kids would go to school hungry, and many families did not even have the necessities of life. These factors contributed to the high crime rates that occurred in many neighborhoods of the West Side. To make matters worse, these overwhelmingly black ghettos were run by white ward officials who actually lived elsewhere but kept their positions by providing so-called ghost addresses within the neighborhood. This pretty much assured that blacks living in the West Side ghettos remained powerless and voiceless. These issues made Chicago an ideal place for a civil rights campaign.

Chicago was not always a segregated city, but the Great Migration of blacks that fled the terror of the South to northern cities led to the dramatic growth in Chicago's African-American population. Blacks thought they were escaping racism and discrimination by leaving the South, but as they settled north, they were met with more racism. As the number of blacks entering Chicago during the 1910s and 1920s increased and crossed tacit racial boundaries, they experienced more threats and violence. Almost 60 homes owned or leased by blacks in white communities were bombed between 1917 and 1921 in an effort to run blacks out of the neighborhood.

In addition to the intimidation and violence, white Chicagoans found other ways to exclude blacks. Neighborhood improvement associations were formed, mostly by the Chicago Real Estate Board (CREB), to pressure white homeowners and realtors against renting or selling to blacks.

Satter reports, "Rather than allowing blacks to purchase property wherever they wished, CREB decided to confine such sales to blocks immediately adjoining neighborhoods that already contained black residents. No new areas would be opened until these blocks became entirely black. Chicago's realtors were thus instrumental in the creation of a dual housing market both locally and nationally—that is, a white market of low prices and expansive neighborhood choices and a black market of high prices and extremely limited options."[111]

Chicago and its real estate policies became innovators for their restrictive and discriminatory policies towards blacks and soon other cities followed suit. A typical restrictive covenant would decree: *At no time shall said premises... be sold, occupied, let or leased... to anyone of any race other than the Caucasian, except that this covenant shall not prevent occupancy by domestic servants of a different race domiciled with an owner or tenant.*[112]

Covenants were also used against Jews and Asians but mostly targeted blacks. The restrictive covenants, combined with the bombings and improvement associations, helped create Chicago's first all-black ghetto on the city's South Side. The violence, discrimination, and segregation worsened as more blacks entered Chicago during and after World War II.
Between 1940 and 1960, Chicago's black population increased from around a quarter million to more than 800,000. Black migrants started settling in areas of the South Side's Black Belt and also in West Side neighborhoods like Lawndale, Garfield Park, Near West Side, and later Austin.

In the 1940s there was a severe housing shortage in Chicago, exacerbated when veterans returned after World War II. During that same time, many white Chicagoans moved to brand new suburban neighborhoods. However, blacks did not have this same luxury.

Sattler notes, "The new suburbs generally excluded them (blacks); similarly, within the city limits most African-Americans who sought to rent or buy outside of the Black Belt or Near West Side were curtly informed by white real estate agents that the apartment or building they had inquired about was no longer available."[113]

Not only did state and city policies affect blacks, but certain federal policies made it even harder for blacks to get a fair deal in housing. The Federal Housing Administration (FHA), which was established in 1934, offered insurance for the home loans financial institutions granted. Being able to obtain cheap and easy loans made it easier for many Americans to buy homes. Back then, mortgages were typically cheaper than paying rent.

The problem was, blacks were almost never allowed to obtain mortgage loans because of FHA policies, which were not supported by any facts demonstrating that blacks would or could not pay their mortgages. In addition, if any blacks moved onto a certain block, the FHA would often refuse to insure mortgages or home improvement loans for the entire block. That gave white homeowners even more incentive to keep blacks off their blocks.

Since African-Americans were excluded from getting a home loan from a bank, many bought houses on contract, which meant the owner acted as the lender. Buyers agreed to a down payment and a specified number of monthly payments as well as other terms designed to benefit the seller. It was essentially a way for real estate agents to exploit African-Americans' inability to purchase mortgages. White real estate predators would inflate the price of a house and then sell it knowing that the black buyer would most likely not be able to pay off the mortgage.

Selling on contract allowed agents to evict the buyer if they missed a single payment. To make matters worse, often times blacks would move into their new home only to find there were many problems with the place. The homeowner would then have to spend extra money trying to fix the never-ending flaws of the home in which they had just purchased. Soon they would be so broke that they could not continue to pay their monthly installments. Real estate exploiters would then evict the homeowner, keeping their deposit and monthly payments.

In the late 1940s, violence increased against blacks who moved into white neighborhoods. Whites would burn and vandalize their houses and come in gangs that led to full-scale riots. In July 1946, a black physician purchased a home in Park Manor, a white South Side neighborhood. In response, a mob of two to three thousand whites set fire to his garage and stoned his building.

That December, the families of two black veterans—John Fort, who had earned four battle stars and fought in the Battle of the Bulge, and Letholian Waddles, who had served in the Philippines—attempted to move into the Airport Homes, a temporary veterans' housing project located in another white South Side area. Chicago Housing Authority officials had hoped that a small percentage of these apartments could be rented to black residents without much controversy. After all, the housing was temporary, for war veterans only, and offered only to tenants who had been rigorously screened. Instead, Fort and Waddles were met by a mob of three thousand whites, who stoned their moving van, burned a cross in front of their building, and resisted police efforts to disperse them.[114]

In August of 1947, five thousand whites rioted for three nights after a small number of black veterans attempted to move into the Fernwood Park Homes, another temporary South Side housing project constructed for veterans. Then five thousand whites spent days looting and tossing Molotov cocktails at a building in suburban Cicero ... where a single unit had been rented to a black family.[115]

Similar violence took place in the originally all-white Trumbull Park housing project and raged on intermittently in years to come. Racial tension was high in Chicago and would spike even higher when Martin Luther King and the SCLC came to Chicago in 1966, with the initial goal of improving the heavy segregation that existed in schools, eventually breaking down the barriers of housing discrimination. His method to accomplish these goals was the same strategy that was successful in the South; nonviolent protests. King and the SCLC hoped to organize Chicagoans into a massive, nonviolent movement to fight racism, discrimination, and segregation.

King was typically embraced by Southerners also looking to end discrimination and segregation, but many Chicagoans did not share the same enthusiasm as his fellow Southern activists, feeling that their problems were different than the challenges blacks faced in the South. Civil rights groups and black pastors believed that King's nonviolent approach would not have a positive impact on the black struggles of Chicago.

Mayor Richard J. Daley had firm control over Chicago. The political machine he ran was extremely efficient in that it assured he would retain power by offering services and favors for votes. Dorothy Tillman from the SCLC compared Daley to a slave master.

"Down south you lived on the plantation, you worked it, and you had your food, clothing, and shelter. Up here they lived on a plantation with Boss Daley as slave master. Their jobs, their clothes, their shelter, food, all that depended on Boss Daley."[116]

The SCLC decided to make their home on the West Side, which was even more desperate and poor than the South Side. King moved into North Lawndale, considered by many the king of all slums in Chicago. North Lawndale is a neighborhood just southeast of Austin Village. Lawndale, like most West Side neighborhoods, had once been mostly white, inhabited by Europeans and Jews.

As King took up residence in one of the rat-infested apartments on Hamlin Avenue, he and the SCLC planned their campaign in Chicago. First, they attempted to desegregate Chicago's schools. The SCLC, however, was met with intense opposition. Every demand made by King and his organization was ignored by Daley's self-appointed superintendent of Chicago's public schools, Benjamin C. Willis. Without being able to make a dent on the segregation of Chicago's public schools, King and the SCLC turned their campaign to target economic injustice and Chicago's ghettos. The SCLC and the Coordinating Committee of Community Organizations (CCCO) of Chicago combined into a joint organization called the Chicago Freedom Movement (CFM).

The CFM scheduled a rally at Soldier Field, the stadium of the Chicago Bears. After the rally, King led a march to Chicago's City Hall and posted the CFM's demands on one of the buildings doors. Some of the demands included desegregation of Chicago's schools, abolition of garnishment and wage assignment, increased garbage collection, street cleaning and building inspection services, ready access to the names of owners and investors for all slum, new public housing outside of the ghetto, the creation of a citizen review board to investigate complaints of police brutality, having all real estate brokers immediately make their listings available on a non-discriminatory basis, endorsement of and support for open occupancy, and the replacement of absentee precinct captains with representatives who actually lived in their districts.[117]

King and civil rights activist Al Raby met with Daley to negotiate the demands of the CFM. The meeting did not go well, and nothing changed. The CFM now knew that they needed to move to the next phase of their movement.

King and the CFM planned to start marching in all-white Chicago neighborhoods. King had long been criticized for inciting violence. He always preached and practiced nonviolent protesting, but it is true that part of his strategy was to provoke white reaction, which would then get national attention and then hopefully force the government to act. This strategy had indeed been very effective in the South.

But before the CFM could act, a riot broke out in the near West Side after police arrested a young man for opening a fire hydrant. A crowd grew and became angry. Local blacks started throwing rocks at police cars, breaking windows, and looting. Reinforcements were called in and a force of over nine hundred, almost all white police officers, tried to regain control. Many complained of police brutality.

"Witnesses described people who were attacked by police as they stepped out of buses or simply tried to walk home from work. Searching for rioters and looters, police pushed their way into houses and beat any inhabitant who protested. Locals reported that the police used vicious racial epithets and seemed to be 'enjoying' the free hand they'd been given."[118]

The riot soon made its way into neighboring Lawndale, where Dr. King had been residing. The National Guard was called in and eventually the riot

92

was suppressed, but only after sixty-one police injuries were reported and over five hundred arrests. Two civilians were killed, including a pregnant fourteen-year- old girl, and many were injured, but this was not mentioned by the media. After the riot, King tried to pull the youth of these neighborhoods together and explain to them that violence was not the answer, and that it was hurting their cause.

King was correct, violence did hurt their cause as Daley blamed the riots on King and his associates. Regardless, the next stage of the movement needed to begin.

The all-white South Side neighborhoods of Marquette Park and Gage Park were strategically chosen as places to march due to data showing numerous acts of racial discrimination. As marches begun in Gage Park, protesters were confronted by whites carrying signs that read: *Nigger Go Home* and *White Power*. White residents also pelted marchers with rocks and bottles. The next day, activists began a march in neighboring Marquette Park where they were met with more hostility and violence. Marchers commented on the upsetting differences in crowds between the North and the South.

> In Chicago, mobbing interracial protesters was a family affair. Little boys waved nooses and chanted, 'I'd love to be an Alabama trooper / That is what I'd really like to be / For if I were an Alabama trooper / Then I could hang a nigger legally.' Ten- year-old girls pelted protesters with whatever objects they could find. Teenagers screamed *White power* and *Burn them like Jews*. Young couples helped each other to rocks for stoning the marchers. Older women seemed particularly venomous. As one marcher recalled, they spat and 'ranged a long list of sexual perversion charges against us. Over fifty of the approximately five hundred marchers had been injured by the mob, as had two police officers. Many more would have been hurt if not for three black street gangs - the Cobras, the Vice Lords, and the Roman Saints - who acted as marshals, 'batting down with their

bare hands hundreds of bricks and bottles.[119]

Many police officers stood by with indifference instead of protecting marchers from violence. This was shown on national TV, which made Daley and the city of Chicago resemble what the nation saw in Birmingham and other Southern towns.

Protests continued in Belmont-Cragin where protesters were actually given adequate protection by police. King took protesters back to Gage Park where more violence and hate ensued with rocks, bricks, bottles, and cherry bombs thrown at protesters. Whites taunted them with shouts of *Cannibals* and *Go home, niggers*. One of the signs read: *The only way to stop niggers is to exterminate them*.

People were holding swastikas in the air and throwing anything they could find at the protesters. At this march, King was hit in the head by a huge rock that knocked him down.

Marches continued for weeks, which put more and more pressure on Daley, who agreed to meet with members of the CFM, desperate to end the protests. He had already issued an injunction to limit marches, which King declared illegal and unconstitutional. The CFM presented their demands to a subcommittee that agreed to many of CFM's demands and passed a ten-point proposal to execute them. Some believed this was a significant accomplishment for Chicago and the Civil Rights Movement, but most were skeptical that the proposal would lead to any real change. The dissatisfied activists then planned for a march in Cicero, where just a couple months earlier a black teenager searching for a job was beaten to death by four white teenagers.

The CFM knew that they would be met with fierce rage if they marched in Cicero, but they decided to protest nonetheless. As expected, the marchers were insulted and abused, but without Dr. King in attendance, many protesters began to shout back and pick up the bricks that were hurled at them and throw them back into the crowd. After the march, many activists felt empowered that they fearlessly marched through one of the most hostile places in Chicago, yet most agreed that there were no real short-term or long-term benefits that resulted from this march.

Momentum of the movement began to weaken and many considered the whole Chicago Campaign a failure. Satter reports that months after the movement, "The AFSCs William Moyer issued a report claiming that there had been virtually no progress in desegregating housing since the summit agreement of August 1966: the city's realtors had continued to discriminate, the CHR had taken no further enforcement action, and there had been no changes in the policies of the Chicago Housing Authority, the Public Aid Department, or the Department of Urban Renewal."[120]

Breaking Chicago's racism and discrimination was like trying to break into Fort Knox.

#

It is inadequate to talk about housing discrimination and segregation of blacks in Chicago without mentioning the dark history of its high-rise public housing. Cabrini-Green, the Robert Taylor Homes, and the Henry Horner Homes became infamous in Chicago for all the wrong reasons. Parts of the horror movie, *Candyman*, were filmed in Cabrini Green. But the horrors that took place in Cabrini-Green for many of the residents there were all too real. Today you won't see any of these notorious high-rises as you travel through Chicago. They have been demolished, displacing thousands of poor, mostly black residents.

The Chicago Housing Authority (CHA) was founded in 1937. This municipal not-for-profit corporation was in charge of developing and creating public housing. Soon after its creation, four public housing projects opened in different parts of the city. Three of these projects were built for low-income whites, and one was built for blacks in a South Side Ghetto. At that time federal law mandated that the tenants of a housing development be the same race as the people in the area it was located.

Years later, there was a brief period in which CHA tried to racially integrate public housing. After receiving significant funding, CHA proposed a plan to build public housing units, mostly high-rises, at different sites across the city. This was met with heavy resistance from whites. Violence and riots broke out in many areas where whites opposed living with or near blacks.

James Loewen explains, "The Chicago Housing Authority (CHA), burned by white resistance to African-Americans who tried to live in Airport Homes after World War II, changed its policies to comply with sundown suburbs and neighborhoods. It built public housing for blacks in black neighborhoods and public housing for whites in white neighborhoods."[121] Thus, CHA was forced to construct most public housing in or near black ghettos.

The Robert Taylor Homes were constructed in the South Side's Bronzeville neighborhood during the same time that the Dan Ryan Expressway was being built. The expressway became an intended division between prosperous white neighborhoods—including Bridgeport where Mayor Daley resided—and the soon-to-be-erected high-rise on the other side of the expressway. This became the largest public housing project in the United States. The Cabrini-Green homes, comprised of both high-rise buildings and row houses, were built in the Near North Side. The Henry Horner homes were built on the Near West Side near what is now called the United Center.

After 1950, the public housing projects began to deteriorate more and more each year. The city, state, and federal governments began to defund high-rise public housing substantially. Many residents of the projects believed that their buildings were being neglected intentionally. They felt they were all segregated into overcrowded buildings and then left to rot and deal with constantly broken elevators, infestations of roaches and rats, drug dealing, gang turf wars, and gun violence. Many youths were sucked up in the gang life that was so prevalent in these area. Some families were afraid to let their kids go outside for fear of them getting shot. In Cabrini-Green, snipers would shoot from the high-rises. Two police officers were gunned down, exacerbating the tension between the police and the residents. Chicago Mayor Jane Byrne temporarily moved into Cabrini-Green to draw attention to the high crime rate in the area. She moved in for three weeks and was surrounded by an army of police the whole time, a luxury the residents did not have.

Public housing residents were subjected to much harassment. First, the screening and application process was rigorous and invasive. Many people applying for public housing were rejected because they did not meet the requirements. Any criminal history would disqualify an applicant on the spot so many families were forced to separate because someone in their family had a criminal history. If anyone with a criminal record was discovered living there, the whole family would be evicted. Housing Authority employees could randomly search homes and residents would be evicted for the smallest of reasons. Residents were also subjected to random drug testing. Police harassment was common, but if residents truly needed help, officers were slow to respond.

In the mid-to-late 1990s, the Department of Housing and Urban Development (HUD) took over from CHA and the Plan for Transformation was announced. The high-rises would be demolished and replaced with mixed- income housing and Section 8 vouchers.

It was clear that the high-rises had to go, not so clear were the mixed feelings of residents who had lived in the buildings for decades. Despite the violence and poverty that was epidemic, many residents felt a sense of community living in the high-rises. They did not like the crime and the deterioration of the housing, but they felt a strong connection to the place where they lived for so long. It was truly bittersweet for many residents as they watched the massive high-rises topple to the ground. Residents were also concerned with the realization that they would be relocated to some place away from all the people and things they knew. Many were promised they could return when construction was finished, but this frequently did not happen. Some former residents qualified for mixed-income living, but most were displaced throughout the city.

As of this writing, if you drive down Cambridge Avenue, between Division and Chicago, you will see small remnants of what used to be Cabrini-Green. The high-rises have been knocked down, most of the row houses have been boarded up, but yet there are still a couple blocks of row houses that resemble how Cabrini-Green used to be. This area has been gentrified with luxurious apartments and condominiums, Starbucks, and nice restaurants. It is prime real estate being sold for big money.

But on Larrabee and Cambridge you can still see the run down row houses and police cameras flashing above them. It appears to be more like a prison than a place to live with fences surrounding the perimeter and neglected parks with decaying basketball hoops. The row houses are occupied by black residents, either descendants of or people that have themselves been part of the Cabrini-Green community for decades.

The kids attend Jenner Elementary School, a school that is underfunded and struggling. I wonder what Cabrini residents think about as their neighborhood has been built up and torn down without having any say in the matter. I also wonder what the new residents think about as they walk over what used to be massive towers and the blood of residents that were taken way too early. Do they even know? Do they care?

#

It should be no surprise to anyone that gangs, drugs, and violence became perpetual problems in the high-rises that occupied the city for so long. The discrimination that existed was debilitating to blacks, but Chicago was not alone in its discriminatory practices across the North. In the 1960s alone, riots erupted in almost all major cities in the North. New York, Philadelphia, Detroit, Watts, Baltimore, Newark, and Milwaukee were only some of the cities that were affected by race riots during the 1960s. Dr. King called riots the language of the unheard, and marginalized African-Americans were tired of being unheard.

After Dr. King was assassinated in 1968, riots emerged in cities all across the North. Chicago was no exception, and the West Side was particularly hit hard. Many people blamed—and still blame—black residents of the South and West Sides for destroying their own neighborhoods. Many believe that the decay and destruction of those neighborhoods was due to the negligent, dirty welfare tenants that occupied properties in those areas and locals who trashed their own neighborhoods during the riots.

The truth, however, is that the violent opposition to blacks by the common citizens of Chicago and the discriminatory housing practices that were enforced by government officials, real estate agents, and landlords played a giant role in creating the poverty and crime that we now see in inner city neighborhoods.

Soon after the North Lawndale and Garfield Park neighborhoods turned black, Austin Village followed. Satter explains, "Profiteering around racial change followed a traditional pattern. As the number of black residents increased in Austin, a Chicago neighborhood west of Lawndale, savings and loan institutions redlined the area."[122]

Speculators in Chicago decided that Austin Village was a prime spot to exploit blacks in order to make a nice profit. They played on racial fears by convincing whites that blacks were infiltrating their neighborhood, which in turn would create destruction and bring down their property values. Whites began fleeing Austin Village, selling their homes for next to nothing. Real estate agents would then hike up the prices of their properties and sell them to blacks on contract.

The number of real estate agents working in Austin went from forty in 1962 to three hundred a decade later. This explains why Austin went from a mostly white neighborhood to a predominately black neighborhood. Austin did not become black because blacks like to stay together as some people wrongly assume; it was intentionally turned black by discriminatory housing practices. As Matthew Desmond notes in his book *Evicted*, "The poor did not crowd into slums because of cheap housing. They were there—and this was especially true of the black poor—simply because they were allowed to be."[123]

All Northern cities practiced methodical, widespread housing discrimination against African-Americans. In *Arc of Justice*, author Kevin Boyle describes the harsh treatment and extensive discrimination that African- Americans faced.

"Whites decided that blacks couldn't live wherever they wanted. They were to be hidden away in a handful of neighborhoods, walled into ghettos. Businessmen infused the real estate market with racist rules and regulations. White landlords wouldn't show black tenants apartments outside the ghetto. White real estate agents wouldn't show them houses in white neighborhoods. Bankers wouldn't offer them mortgages. Insurance agents wouldn't provide them with coverage. Developers wrote legal restrictions into their deeds, barring blacks from new housing tracts.... Those who had no black neighbors organized to keep their areas lily-white. They formed legal organizations-protective associations, they called them- to write clauses into their deeds prohibiting the sale of their homes to blacks.... And if a black family somehow managed to breach the defenses, they could always drive them out, quietly if possible, violent if necessary."[124]

In *Ghetto* Mitchell Duneier adds: "Isolation from mainstream society, as well as the decrepitude caused by overcrowding, produced notorious conditions, behaviors, and traits that could gradually be invoked to rationalize further negative attitudes and more extreme isolation. The consequences of ghettoization provided an apparent justification for the original condition."[125]

So not only did racist whites create black ghettos, but they now use the violence and despair that persists inside those ghettos as a cruel justification to maintain them.

Today, ghettos are still being exploited and poor blacks are trapped inside a new form of slavery. A lack of resources and opportunities limit them from ever escaping the invisible, but impenetrable, walls of ghetto life. They are stuck in a vicious cycle of poverty, discrimination, and violence.

Desmond illustrates the housing crisis of eviction and how it tears apart poor families. "Today, the majority of poor renting families in America spend over half of their income on housing, and at least one in four dedicates over 70 percent to paying the rent and keeping the lights on.... Millions of Americans are evicted every year because they can't make rent.... If incarceration had come to define the lives of men from impoverished black neighborhoods, eviction was shaping the lives of women. Poor black men were locked up. Poor black women were locked out."[126]

Once you are evicted it goes on your record and follows with you like a scarlet letter. Landlords typically deny families that have an eviction on record. If you have a criminal record, your chances of being accepted into a housing rental are lower. Blacks have an even tougher time getting approved because of the color of their skin. Poor renters, especially poor black women, get stuck in an endless cycle of poverty and despair.

Desmond explains that landlords and property management companies try "to avoid discriminating by setting clear criteria and holding all applicants to the same standards. But equal treatment in an unequal society could still foster inequality. Because black men were disproportionately incarcerated and black women disproportionately evicted, uniformly denying housing to applicants with recent criminal or eviction records still had an incommensurate impact on African-Americans."[127]
The result is that they ended up having to rent neglected housing in dangerous areas with few economic opportunities because those are the only units where they are accepted. Then because these units usually are hardly adequate to live, they have to pay additional money to fix the countless repairs in their dilapidated units. A cut in hours or a sudden firing leaves them with no money to pay the rent, resulting in eviction, and the cycle continues.

In addition to discrimination in renting, Hispanic and African-American neighborhoods were targeted by the subprime lending industry that conned renters into bad mortgages and encouraged homeowners to refinance under risky terms. People of all colors were affected by predatory real estate agents and toxic loans leading to the 2008 economic crash, but black families were hardest hit, losing 31 percent of their wealth. The housing crisis led to thousands of foreclosures, affecting minorities the most.

Black residents of Chicago and many other cities were intentionally segregated into ghettos and cheated out of a chance to start a life with the opportunities that are essential to all human beings. Many now live in segregated ghettos where violence, poverty, and discrimination continue as a harsh reality of daily life.

Segregating poor minorities into an isolated area is never a recipe for success. But when you add unjust policies and laws to this already desperate situation, it's like pouring salt on an open wound.

#

It's a hot summer evening, and I am riding my bike with a bunch of strangers across a town that most people avoid: Austin. I'm riding with a group known as Slow Roll Chicago. This organization assembles a group of cyclists who slowly ride through poor, marginalized neighborhoods on the West and South Sides of Chicago. The goals of this organization is to ensure that all neighborhoods have equal access to bikes and to promote a healthy, active lifestyle.

I look around Austin and see African-Americans and run down houses. I see vacant houses boarded up that at one time had so much potential. I also have to make sure not to look up for too long, or I may dive into a crater on the road, which used to be a pot hole. I'm a bit perplexed at what I am feeling. I feel joy as I see kids and adults smiling, waving, and encouraging this strange group of people slowly biking through their neighborhood. I also feel sadness as I see foreclosed properties and roads that would be more fitting in a Third World country. I feel anguish as I wonder how many of these black children will lose someone they know to gang violence? I ponder how many of them will join a gang, or become addicted to drugs. How many of these smiling, innocent children that are waving at me, will end up in prison, or have to grow up without a father because he is behind bars or a victim of violence?

I let these feelings sink in as Slow Roll Chicago and I pass across Austin Boulevard back into Oak Park, where I see one beautiful, million-dollar house after another. I then spot two white children sitting on their deck playing with their phones. I start to think how drastically different their life is now, and will most likely be in the future, from the kids I had just seen on the other side of Austin Boulevard. Whatever obstacles they have to overcome are very different from the massive hurdles that kids on the other side of Austin Boulevard have to conquer.

The two kids in Oak Park do not have to worry about crossing into gang territory as they walk to school in Oak Park. They are not concerned about wearing certain colors to avoid conflicts with gangs. They do not have the need or pressure to join a gang. They most likely do not have a parent or sibling in prison or dead from gun violence. They probably will receive a better education. They most likely will have the money to pay for college. And they are more likely to have connections for employment. It is baffling to think of the drastic outcomes of two lives simply based on the side of Austin Boulevard that they were born on.

To be sure, this does not mean that all kids in Austin will join a gang or go to jail. It also does not mean that all kids in Oak Park have it easy and will not have to overcome obstacles to achieve success. There are many kids in Austin that will overcome insurmountable odds and live a very successful life. There are also kids in Oak Park that are extremely gifted and have a strong work ethic that will play a big role in their future. But it cannot be denied that the opportunities that kids in Oak Park and other middle to upper class neighborhoods have are more abundant than those who live in Austin or other low-income, crime-infested neighborhoods.

The mixed emotions I felt when cruising through Austin left me with the contrary feelings of both despair and hope. Despair that poor minorities have been discriminated against and neglected for centuries, but hope that the strength and determination that I observe in the people of Austin, and all across the country, will keep fighting for justice and change.

The War on the Poor, the Rise of the Prison Industrial Complex

America's public enemy #1 in the United States is drug abuse. ~ Richard Nixon

Just say no. Drugs are bad. Drug addicts are weak, repulsive creatures. Drug users need to be punished. Drugs need to be eliminated from planet Earth.

These statements are typical of how many feel about drugs and drug users. Many people view drugs as the very root of the destruction and deterioration of neighborhoods, cities, countries, and the people living in them. After all, people choose to do and sell drugs and therefore should be punished for their lack of judgment and strength, right? And the only way we can cure our society and citizens from their destructive choices is to jail all the offenders and eventually exterminate drugs from the world.

Or is it?

After the progress and turmoil of the Civil Rights Era, America needed a new way to marginalize and control minorities, especially blacks. However, this would not be as effortless as it had been in previous decades. Public opinion was changing. It was not publicly accepted to promote racism and discrimination anymore. Most blacks could now legally vote and attend the same public facilities and schools as whites. There would not be politicians publicly demanding segregation now and forever like George Wallace had done. So politicians needed to adapt to the current trends of the post-Civil Rights United States. And adapt they did.

The political situation shifted significantly to the right as Richard Nixon took office in 1969. Nixon declared drug abuse public enemy number one and coined the term *war on drugs*. But was this really when the war on drugs began?

Johann Hari traces the drug war back to its original roots in his intriguing book, *Chasing the Scream*. Prior to 1914, drugs were legal and opiates were readily available at any pharmacy and in products: Coca-Cola was made from the coca plant. In the early part of the twentieth century, drugs became associated with crime and minorities. Many believed that the prevalence of crime was due to blacks using drugs and then committing heinous crimes like rape and murder. Mexican and Chinese immigrants were also blamed for the supposed increase in drugs and crime.

After much propaganda, the United States passed the Harrison Narcotics Tax Act in 1914. Sixteen years later the Federal Bureau of Narcotics would be established and President Herbert Hoover's administration appointed Harry Anslinger to lead it.

Anslinger had a real disdain for narcotics and African-Americans. He also had a problem: the agency did not have a lot of support. Although the Federal Bureau of Narcotics was just established, it was really an extension of the former Department of Prohibition, which was dwindling as Prohibition was coming to a close, and recognized as a failure. Harry needed support and he needed it fast. So he combined the two things he most despised, drugs and blacks, and proposed the idea that when blacks were on drugs, they could not be controlled.

This played well into the fears of most Americans. Even though there was no proof that blacks were using drugs more than whites, and that the ones who were using became violent and attacked whites, Anslinger's strategy began to work. He started getting more and more support and with this support came money, which gave him power and influence. Soon, the drug war was underway and barreled ahead with tremendous speed. The war on drugs would expand to a global conflict, which is still going strong now, over a hundred years later.

Fast forward to Ronald Reagan's presidential campaign. He condemned blacks and other poor minorities, but he did so in a much more discrete way than prior politicians. In *The Jim Crow* Michelle Alexander explains, "Reagan mastered the 'excision of the language of race from conservative public discourse' and thus built on the success of earlier conservatives who developed a strategy of exploiting racial hostility or resentment for political gain without making explicit reference to race.... Condemning 'welfare queens' and criminal 'predators,' he (Reagan) rode into office with the strong support of disaffected whites - poor and working-class whites who felt betrayed by the Democratic Party's embrace of the civil rights agenda."[128]

Many politicians were berating welfare recipients as lazy people who did not want to work and instead preferred to live off the government. Although people of all colors were on welfare, blacks were the intended target. Propaganda suggesting that blacks were criminals was also used to turn poor and working class whites against impoverished blacks. Reagan backed up his campaign rhetoric of fighting crime and drugs by declaring his administration's war on drugs shortly after taking office in 1982, even though less than 2 percent of the American public considered drugs as the most important issue facing the United States.

Reagan's plan was to decrease federal spending in areas that he did not value—like social services and drug treatment, prevention, and education—and increase funding for programs that were aligned with his conservative beliefs, such as antidrug programs.

The new and improved war on drugs had new life.

Reagan had to justify the need for more law enforcement and money to fund the war on drugs he was raging, despite the fact that drugs were not on the rise and were not even considered a major problem by most of the public.

Kristian Williams, author of *Our Enemies in Blue*, says the same attention was not given to driving under the influence.

> Consider drunk driving: In the mid-80s, at about the same time legislators were establishing draconian sentences for small amounts of crack cocaine, they were also setting minimum sentences for driving under the influence. The juxtaposition is revealing. At the time, drunk driving killed about 22,00 people each year, which was more than all other drug-related deaths combined. But while crack was tagged with a five-year minimum sentence, the penalty for drunk driving was typically two days for a first offense, up to ten days for a

second. The difference is that, while 93 percent of those convicted of possessing crack are black 78 percent of those arrested from drunk driving were white men.[129]

Facts, of course, never really mattered. The war on drugs was going to be fought regardless of the truth. So Reagan waged a fierce media campaign to convince the public that drugs were a major problem in America. The media offensive aimed at instilling fear in Americans. It played on the fear many whites already possessed: that blacks and other minorities were dangerous criminals and needed to be stopped at any cost. When crack cocaine hit the streets in the mid '80s, the scare tactics of the media would further label blacks as menacing, crack-addicted criminals.

The crack epidemic hit inner cities at a particularly vulnerable time. Most blacks that lived in urban areas had blue collar, factory jobs. During and after World War II, industrial jobs were in high demand, but as jobs went overseas and advanced technology eliminated many factory jobs in the 1970s, many blacks were left unemployed. African-Americans living in inner cities were isolated and had limited access to transportation. This prevented them from seeking employment in the suburbs, where many of the jobs were now located. They also were less educated due to the discrimination discussed in earlier chapters. These factors combined resulted in high unemployment for those in inner city neighborhoods. So crack was an opportunity for desperate, unemployed blacks to make money.

Crack became a hot topic that the media could not resist. Alexander notes, "Thousands of stories about the crack crisis flooded the airwaves and newsstands, and the stories had a clear racial subtext. The articles typically featured black crack whores, crack babies, and gangbangers, reinforcing already prevalent racial stereotypes of black women as irresponsible, selfish welfare queens, and black men as predators—part of an inferior and criminal subculture."[130]

Now that Reagan and the media had clearly defined the enemy, it was time to attack.

By 1986 there was a strong consensus in America that the drug issue needed to be addressed aggressively. The get-tough-on-crime movement was in full swing. Congress allocated more money to the antidrug crusade, enlisted the military in the narcotics control efforts, the death penalty was given for some drug-related crimes, and courts allowed illegally obtained evidence to be admitted in drug trials. In addition, legislation introduced mandatory minimum sentences for certain drug offenses. So for example, a person convicted of cocaine possession without the intent to sell automatically received a five-year minimum sentence, even if it was their first offense.

New legislation also allowed public housing authorities to evict any tenant that allowed or enabled any form of drug-related activity to occur in or near public housing. Federal benefits, including student loans, were rescinded for anyone convicted of a drug offense.

When George H.W. Bush became president in 1988, he continued where Reagan left off, opposing affirmative action and civil rights while carrying on the war on drugs with tenacity. By now, it was expected that Republicans would fight vigilantly to uphold the war on drugs and the tough on crime policies, but the stance that Bill Clinton took was not as expected.

Clinton campaigned on being even tougher on crime than his predecessors. It was reported that to prove how tough he was on crime, Clinton flew to Arkansas to watch a severely mentally-impaired, black man be executed. After the execution, Clinton said, "I can be nicked a lot, but no one can say I'm soft on crime."

Clinton intended to prove just how tough he was on crime as he advocated for the three strikes law, which called for harsh mandatory sentences for third felony convictions. As president, Clinton passed a $30 million crime bill that allowed for the expansion of prisons and police forces. Clinton dramatically cut welfare and food stamp funding and also banned convicted drug felons from these benefits. During Clinton's presidency, he cut funding for public housing by $17 billion (a 61 percent decrease) and boosted corrections by $19 billion (a 171 percent increase). Alexander called the construction of prisons the United States' main housing program for the urban poor under Clinton.

The three strikes mandatory minimum sentences were devastating to many, but especially harmful to African-Americans. Being black also made it twice as likely to receive a mandatory minimum sentence than being white. All of this disproportionally affected poor minorities, especially blacks, in ways that many families and whole communities never fully recovered from.

Now that funding and public support were sufficient, a *New York Times*/CBS News Poll indicated that 64 percent of those polled now believed that drugs were the biggest problem in the United States as opposed to just 2 percent seven years earlier. The next step was to give law enforcement free reign to enforce the extremely punitive drug laws. The Fourth Amendment's protection against unreasonable searches and seizures essentially became void. What became known as the stop-and-frisk rule was used by police to stop and search anyone who they deemed suspicious.

Stop and frisk was upheld as constitutional by the Supreme Court in Terry v. Ohio. The majority rules that so long as a police officer has "reasonable articulable suspicion"' that someone is engaged in criminal activity and dangerous, it is constitutionally permissible to stop, question, and frisk that person, even in the absence of probable cause. In essence the ruling gave police officers carte blanche to pull just about anyone over, for just about any reason, as long as they claimed the person was reasonably suspicious—driving while black was perhaps the most suspicious reason of all—and search them for drugs.

Another way police could justify stopping someone was pretext stops. In *Whren v. United States* the Supreme Court held, "the temporary detention of a motorist upon probable cause to believe that he has violated the traffic laws does not violate the Fourth Amendment's prohibition against unreasonable seizures, even if a reasonable officer would not have stopped the motorist absent some additional law enforcement objective."

In other words, an officer can use minor traffic violations as an excuse, or pretext, to search for drugs, even if there isn't a shred of evidence suggesting the motorist was breaking any drug law. Although the person being stopped needs to give consent before the officer can search the person or their vehicle, this can easily be manipulated. For one, many people are unaware that they can refuse consent to a search. An officer can also use his authority to intimidate or trick the person into an unwarranted search.

Even if the person being stopped does not give their consent, they can still be arrested and taken to jail. Police also can bring drug-sniffing dogs to search the vehicle after not receiving consent. In fact, the Drug Enforcement Agency (DEA) actually provides training to the police in how to become more effective when engaging in stop-and-frisk searches.

One may wonder what incentive do police officers and police departments have to enforce such punitive drug policies? When Reagan launched his drug war, law enforcement also did not believe drugs were a major concern and saw an emphasis on minor drug busts as a waste of their time when they could be fighting more serious crime. So in order to get law enforcement onboard with Reagan, the police were essentially bribed. The government basically said to law enforcement: If you fight the war on drugs with us, we'll reward you with money. And a lot of it. This meant that police departments could get new equipment such as helicopters and bulletproof gear, more training, intelligence, and support. Plus officers would get more overtime pay. That gave law enforcement a big green incentive to fight Washington's drug war.

So apparently, if the police wanted to raid a frat house in possession of a lethal combination of Keystone Light and weed, they could do so by surrounding Kappa Sigma with tanks, helicopters, and a police force armed with grenade launchers, automatic weapons, and night-vision goggles. Although this is a fictitious example, the truth was not far off.

Originally Special Weapons and Tactics (SWAT) teams were formed so law enforcement had a specialized trained team to combat and defuse emergencies, like hostage situations or riots. They originated in the 1960s and were used sparingly in the '60s and '70s. But as police agencies became loaded with money, SWAT teams took on a new form. SWAT teams, now equipped with military gear and military training, were used more and more frequently beyond for emergency situations.

The New Jim Crow notes that in 1972, "there were just a few hundred paramilitary drug raids per year in the United States. By the early 1980s, there were three thousand annual SWAT deployments, by 1996 there were thirty thousand, and by 2001 there were forty thousand."[131]

Radley Balko, author of the brilliant book, Rise of the Warrior Cop, believes SWAT teams are "increasingly used as a first option to apprehend people who aren't dangerous at all. Aggressive, SWAT-style tactics are now used to raid neighborhood poker games, doctor's offices, bars and restaurants, and head shops, despite the fact that the targets of these raids pose little threat to anyone."[132]

SWAT teams were used even more frequently and haphazardly after George Bush Jr. and Barack Obama were able to justify their need to fight terrorism post 9/11 although most of the money and equipment given to law enforcement agencies was not used to fight terrorism, but used for the war on drugs. One thing's for sure, police departments had more than enough money and incentive to wage a war on drugs in areas where there was really no war to fight.

Police departments were content to fight the politicians' war on drugs as long as the money and equipment kept flooding in. And fight they did. In 1970, there was one measly SWAT team in the United States, but that number ballooned up to 30,000 twenty-five years later; in 2005 there were between 50,000–60,000 SWAT teams across the United States. There was even a SWAT team in the Consumer Product Safety Commission, in case someone broke in and tried to deregulate the sale and manufacturing of all cribs in the United States. SWAT teams attracted all kinds of people. I mean, who wouldn't want to dress up like a Navy SEAL, kick down doors, and rip a house apart while cursing and throwing people to the ground?

Teenagers in Oak Park

Young boy in Austin

Closed school in Austin

Oak Park River Forest High School

Vacant house on Central Avenue in Austin

Home in Oak Park across from Austin Gardens

Most incarcerated block in Chicago in 2011 - Adams Street in Chicago's
Austin neighborhood

Memorial on Chicago Avenue in Austin

Young man protesting gun violence in Austin

Martin Luther King's former residence in North Lawndale during the Civil Rights Campaign in Chicago

Corner store on 15th and Pulaski

Garage sale on Chicago's West Side

"Luxury Apartments" on Chicago's West Side

Remnants of Freedom Square on Chicago's West Side

Signs of hope on 16th street in North Lawndale

Neighborhood watch in Austin

In all seriousness, being a member of a SWAT team and conducting raids was a dangerous and necessary job. The problem, however, was that SWAT teams were being used more and more for minor drug busts. The Minneapolis, Minnesota, SWAT team was deployed on no-knock warrants thirty-five times in 1986, but in 1996 that same team was deployed for drug raids more than seven hundred times. These minor busts could have easily been accomplished in a less confrontational and aggressive way. But then again, police departments were basically given all of this support and equipment for free, so they may have felt obligated to use it.

The police were also under a tremendous amount of pressure from politicians who were endorsing the war to produce numbers that indicated that the war on drugs was not only necessary but also being won. This meant that law enforcement agencies would have to take manpower away from units that actually fight serious crime and instead delegate them to fighting the war on drugs in order to ensure they were receiving the numbers politicians expected.

Another incentive was that the police could also use the confiscated money and other assets for their own purposes. A report commissioned by the Department of Justice found that between 1988 and 1992 alone drug task forces seized over $1 billion in assets. Plus, that amount of money only represents one federal agency fighting the war on drugs.

Another reason for the drastic increase in drug arrests and raids was the effortlessness of obtaining a search warrant. Many judges were so overloaded with pending drug cases and the sheer volume of search warrants, that they would merely skim through affidavits and approve them without asking questions. Even when judges went through the affidavits more thoroughly, they were rarely denied. Police could also lie or stretch the truth in order to secure a search warrant.

In addition to this, there was fundamentally no accountability if police injured or killed a person. It wasn't uncommon for SWAT teams to mistakenly conduct a raid on the wrong house or find no drugs at that location. Even when botched raids happened, police could ransack a house, tear gas the suspects, and kill a couple dogs—and in some cases people—without even issuing so much as an apology. Thus, the police could act with almost complete impunity.

Often SWAT drug raids were conducted after a supposedly reliable confidential informant (CI) pointed out a suspect or a property that was involved in drugs. But CIs could be unreliable because they had a good incentive to lie; they typically became a CI to reduce a sentence or for other favors, like cash. These raids were terrifying for the victims. SWAT teams usually entered a house in the middle of the night by kicking down doors, spraying tear gas, screaming, and detaining suspects aggressively.

Raids were typically conducted in marginalized neighborhoods where the drug war was being waged most fiercely, meaning the raids and arrests would affect the most vulnerable people; about 80 percent of criminal defendants do not have the means to hire a lawyer. The lack of quality legal representation and the threat of a lengthy sentence pressure many defendants into making a plea bargain that results in prison, jail, or probation. A defendant with the ability to obtain a lawyer is more likely to be released from jail.

A defendant without the means to acquire a lawyer is appointed a public defender. The problem here is that public defenders are overworked and underpaid. Michelle Alexander observes, "Sometimes defenders have well over one hundred clients at a time; many of these clients are facing decades behind bars or life imprisonment. Too often the quality of court-appointed counsel is poor because the miserable working conditions and low pay discourage good attorneys from participating in the system. And some states deny representation to impoverished defendants on the theory that somehow they should be able to pay for a lawyer, even though they are scarcely able to pay for food or rent."[133]

Many defendants have gone weeks, months, or in extreme cases, years without receiving legal representation. When they finally are able to meet with their court appointed lawyer, it's for a very limited amount of time because public defenders have outrageously large caseloads. This means that the overwhelmed defendant will have to make a quick decision that could drastically impact the rest of their lives.

Defendants are typically encouraged to make a plea deal, which is foregoing a trial by submitting a guilty plea in exchange for some form of sentencing leniency. The vast majority of criminal cases are resolved through plea bargains. Because of the harsh mandatory minimum drug laws, many defendants choose to take the plea deal, even if they are innocent, in order to receive a reduced sentence. It may sound outrageous that an innocent person will plead guilty to a crime that they did not commit, but when they are looking at a mandatory minimum sentence of five, 10, or 20 years, or even a possible life sentence, it's easier to understand why many defendants would agree to a reduced sentence.

#

The excessive drug laws and policies, the enforcement by police, and the failure of the courts have all resulted in what is now being called the prison- industrial complex. The growth of prisons and the people condemned to live in them has grown in ways that would have seemed unfathomable 30 years ago.

Michelle Alexander writes, "In less than thirty years, the US penal population exploded from around 300,000 to more than two million, with drug convictions accounting for the majority of the increase. The United States now has the highest rate of incarceration in the world, dwarfing the rates of nearly every developed country, even surpassing those in highly repressive regimes like Russia, China, and Iran. In Germany, 93 people are in prison for every 100,000 adults and children. In the United States, the rate is roughly eight times that, or 750 per 100,000."[134]

To be compared to China, Russia, and Iran for just about anything is never a good thing. Furthermore, the comparison is weak because the United States in fact, incarcerates substantially more of its citizens at a higher rate. To be clear, the United States incarcerates more of its own citizens than Iran, a country whose preferred method of execution is stoning; China, a country who executes more of its citizens than any other country; and Russia, a country that is so repressive that you can't even make a sneeze that sounds like Putin without the possibility of getting thrown in jail for treason. But perhaps the most troubling statistics are those that show who is most affected by mass incarceration and what crime most significantly caused the increase in the prison population.

Minorities—in particular African-Americans—have been affected disproportionately by mass incarceration. By the time Reagan left office in 1989, blacks outnumbered whites in prisons for the first time. The US had more black males in prison than South Africa under apartheid. As law enforcement scooped up blacks at alarming rates, the crimes that they were most commonly being arrested for were drug offenses, which accounted for a 66 percent increase in the federal inmate population and more than half of the increase of state prisoners between 1985 and 2000. In 2012 around a half million people were incarcerated for drug offense compared to an estimated 41,1000 in 1980. Ironically, a high percentage of these convictions were for marijuana, which as of 2016 is legal for recreational use in four states plus the District of Columbia, and more than a dozen more states are expected to legalize shortly.

Once a person is convicted of a felony, their opportunities to succeed are reduced significantly. A convicted felon cannot vote or serve on a jury. They are not eligible for public housing or food stamps, have to acknowledge their criminal history on employment applications, and will be ineligible for a wide range of professional licenses.

If a goal of incarceration is to rehabilitate prisoners into law abiding citizens and prepare them for a life in society, it has failed miserably. Prison life is about survival not rehabilitation. Most prisoners are subjected to inhumane conditions and treatment. They are also surrounded by other criminals, which can make even the most law-abiding citizen become a criminal in that environment. Once they are thrown back into society—where they have most likely lost their job, their place of residence, support from family and friends, and other means to proactively reintegrate into society— they are almost forced back into a life where crime is the only opportunity they have to make money. It's no surprise then that two-thirds of ex-cons are arrested for new crimes—mostly drug offenses and other nonviolent crimes— within three years of their release or parole.

If a former prisoner is released on parole, they have an even higher chance of being sent back to prison. Probationers and parolees are under strict rules and limitations, depending on the crime they have committed. For example, they may be sent to prison if they associate with another felon or break any travel restrictions. In 1980 parole violations accounted for 1 percent of incarceration; in 2000 that number was 35 percent. And of those, two-thirds were sent back to jail for technical violations including unemployment, missing appointments with their parole officer, or failing a drug test. A 2009 Colorado study showed that black parolees were eight times more likely to have their parole revoked by the parole board than white parolees.

The entire system is not conducive to successfully transitioning formerly incarcerated individuals back into society. The system does however, ensure felons to a second-class citizenship where the odds of them returning to prison are high.

Incarceration does not only affect the prisoners who are locked up behind bars. Entire families are affected, a disproportionate number of them black. One in 40 children in the United States has a parent in prison, for black kids, it's one in 15. The increasing prevalence of kids who are growing up with a parent in prison is discouraging, especially when considering the trauma these kids experience makes them far more likely to have significant emotional and social problems. Studies suggest these children are also more likely to become drug or alcohol abusers and commit crime. They may also join a gang to fill the need for an emotional connection or sense of belonging.

Maya Schenwar, author of *Locked Down, Locked Out*, reports, "Boys whose parents are incarcerated are five times more likely to become incarcerated themselves, and kids of prisoners are more likely to go to prison than to graduate from high school.... Many of the 1.7 million children with parents in prison simply haven't learned to write yet."[135]

By locking up so many Americans, especially people who are in prison for nonviolent crimes, we are increasing the likelihood that children with incarcerated parents will repeat their parents' mistakes, thus ensuring a never ending cycle of crime and punishment.

I personally, have always thought that blacks used and sold drugs more than whites. Why wouldn't I? I knew that blacks were arrested frequently for drug possession and selling. The media was always telling me about crackheads and crack babies that were widespread in black ghettos. I even saw with my own two eyes, blacks selling drugs openly on street corners. But after reading and studying the facts, I learned a very different story.

Blacks and Latinos are arrested more frequently for drug violations than whites. That part is true; but I was not aware that whites use and sell drugs at an equal or higher rate than blacks. There have even been studies that found white students use crack significantly more than their black counterparts. Despite these facts black men are incarcerated on drug charges exponentially more than white men. Why?

One reason is living conditions. Many suburbs are inhabited by middle to upper class whites who have big houses where they can use and sell drugs in privacy. On the other hand, many blacks are confined to poor, inner city neighborhoods where they use and deal drugs on the street because they have dilapidated and overcrowded houses or apartments. So it's easier for the police to arrest blacks who are in possession of drugs on the street, rather than whites who are behind closed doors. The police can also stop and frisk and arrest poor minorities because they do not have the power to fight back.

Wealthier whites are more able to hire a lawyer or have another connection to fight unconstitutional searches by the police. Therefore, law enforcement is more vulnerable to repercussions when arresting in wealthier areas. The same principle contributes to the frequency of drug raids in poor areas. If the police injure, kill, or vandalize a house in a wealthy neighborhood when conducting a drug raid, they are more likely to have a lawsuit filed against them. If the police have to get their drug stats up to please politicians, the easiest way to do this is by targeting the weakest and most vulnerable citizens.

Biases also play a large part in who gets arrested and thrown in jail. A survey taken in 1995 and published by the *Journal of Alcohol and Drug Education*, shows the startling results of who Americans picture as drug users. When asked: *Close your eyes for a second, envision a drug user, and describe that person to me,* 95 percent of respondents pictured a black drug user, while only 5 percent imaged other racial groups.

Michelle Alexander cites another study that "involved a video game that placed photographs of white and black individuals holding either a gun or other object (such as a wallet, soda can, or cell phone) into various photographic backgrounds. Participants were told to decide as quickly as possible whether to shoot the target. Consistent with earlier studies, participants were more likely to mistake a black target armed when he was not, and mistake a white target as unarmed, when in fact he was armed."[136]

This also can explain why blacks are shot by police at alarming rates when in many instances they are holding nothing at all or something that vaguely resembles a gun.

Everyone has biases. It is impossible not to, especially because we know the influence the media has on the public. For decades and decades, the media has been instrumental in exposing racial fears in the public. Malcolm X said, "The media's the most powerful entity on earth. They have the power to make the innocent guilty and to make the guilty innocent, and that's power. Because they control the minds of the masses."

As a result of intentional and unintentional influence of politicians and the corporate media, the public has been brainwashed into thinking African- Americans, especially those in ghettos, are criminals. Studies suggest people— from police to jurors—become increasingly harsh when a defendant is stereotypically black and more lenient when the defendant appears more stereotypically white. This is true of jurors as well as law enforcement officers.

Once arrested, race has proven to be a factor in convicting the defendant and the severity of the sentence. For example, blacks are more likely to receive the death penalty than whites for the same crime in certain states. The race of the victim also heavily influenced the decision of whether to impose the death penalty. The Baldus study reviewed murder cases in Georgia and found defendants charged with killing white victims received the death penalty eleven times more often than defendants charged with killing black victims. Georgia prosecutors sought the death penalty in 70 percent of cases involving black defendants and white victims, but only in 19 percent of cases involving white defendants and black victims.

In the *McCleskey v. Kemp*, the Supreme Court upheld the death penalty sentencing of Warren McCleskey for armed robbery and murder, saying the racially disproportionate impact in the Georgia death penalty indicated by the Baldus study was not enough to overturn the guilty verdict without showing a "racially discriminatory purpose." So even as blacks were being arrested at rates far exceeding whites and being convicted and sentenced more frequently and harshly, there was basically nothing that they could do in the courtroom to show discrimination was pervasive.

Another discriminatory practice was the unjust sentencing of crack convictions. As the crack epidemic hit the inner cities, blacks became the majority of convicted crack offenders while whites were the bulk of the convicted cocaine offenders. Crack and cocaine both come from the same plant, but are made differently. Crack has been said to be the more addictive of the two. It is also the cheaper of the two, which made it popular in inner city neighborhoods. Although crack is the more dangerous of the two drugs, the effects both drugs have on the body in the long-term are destructive. Any differences in the drugs do not justify the inequity of sentences.

For example, a conviction for selling five hundred grams of powder cocaine might carry a five-year mandatory sentence, while only five grams of crack triggers the same sentence. Today, the difference in the ratio of crack to cocaine sentences is not as extreme, yet sentences for crack offenses are still more punitive than cocaine offenses. As hard as we try to believe that we live in a society that is no longer racist, the statistics and facts show otherwise.

If crime and drug use were declining due to the punitive policies that were, and still are, being used, one could at least justify the need for them. However, there is no evidence that suggests that there are fewer drug users, sellers, or that the overall number of drugs in the United States has decreased. There is also no proof that crime has been reduced. In fact, many studies show that crime and drug abuse have increased since the war on drugs.

Professor Jeffrey Miron of Harvard University notes that the murder rate has dramatically increased twice in US history: The first was 1920 to 1933 during Prohibition. The second was from 1970 to 1990, when the war on drugs was escalated.

When the United States prohibited alcohol in 1920, it created a thriving business opportunity for anyone who was tough and bold enough. The rise of John Torrio, Arnold Rothstein, Al Capone, and many others was facilitated by Prohibition because it gave bootleggers the opportunity to make millions of dollars by providing alcohol, which many people still desired.

Johann Hari explains, "When a popular product is criminalized, it does not disappear. Instead, criminals start to control the supply and sale of the product. They have to get it into the country, transport it to where it's wanted, and sell it on the street. At every stage, their product is vulnerable. If somebody comes along and steals it, they can't go to the police or the courts to get it back. So they only defend their property one way: by violence"[137]

Violence would break out over territory, profits, and competition. Everyone was fighting to have the biggest hand in the illegal business of acquiring and selling alcohol and conflicts were usually resolved by violence. When drugs were declared illegal by the Harrison Act in 1914, the same phenomenon took place. All of the sudden, drugs that were previously sold at the pharmacy, were now sold by people on the streets.

Violence escalated substantially starting in the 1970s after the war on drugs was intensified. As heavier drugs were hitting the streets and inner city neighborhoods deteriorated, gangs fought over territory. The money in drugs was so lucrative that everybody wanted a hand in. Gangs now fight over the same things they fought over back in Capone's heyday: territory, money, intimidation, and management.

One would think that the sheer volume of drugs and the number of people using them would have decreased as they became illegal. However, this did not happen. Illegal drugs continue to be used at a high rate, and there is no end in sight. Despite all the families that have been torn apart by the war on drugs and mass incarceration, all of the money spent to fight this war and to build prisons to hold its victims, all the people that have been murdered in the name of the war on drugs, many politicians are still fighting this winless war, and too much of the public supports their fight.

#

As Barack Obama's presidency reaches its final stages as the first black president of the United States, what legacy does he leave behind? Was he the new Martin Luther King that was going to lead blacks to the Promised Land'? Not quite.

Social activist, author, and philosopher Cornel West, when asked on Democracy Now! how Obama's legacy compares to infamous civil rights leaders, asserted, "People think that somehow Barack Obama is the culmination of Frederick Douglass and Martin and Malcolm and Ida and Ella and others, and it's the exact opposite, that he is as establishmentarian, he is as much pro-status quo, as a Bill Clinton or a Hillary Clinton or any other neoliberal opportunist."

As Obama was campaigning for president, he appealed to many progressives. He stood in front of the people and promised that he would break up the big banks, get the United States out of wars, be more transparent, and reform the criminal justice system. It appeared he is opposed to the war on drugs and targeting African-Americans for mass incarceration. All this talk was great. Obama was able to articulate many of the problems facing this country and African-Americans in particular. Unfortunately, it was a lot of bark and not much bite.

After taking office, Obama surrounded himself with many advocates of the war on drugs. With that came punitive punishments that coincide with waging the war. In fact, Obama's vice president Joe Biden was a strong advocate for the war on drugs and the expansion of the prison-industrial complex.

In his book *Wages of Rebellion*, Pulitzer Prize-winning journalist and author Chris Hedges explains, "The Omnibus Crime Bill, pushed through the Senate with the help of Joe Biden, appropriated $30 billion to expand the nation's prison program, state and local law enforcement, and border patrols over a six-year period. It gave $10.8 billion in federal matching funds to local governments to hire 100,000 new police officers over five years. It provided nearly $10 billion for the construction of new federal prisons. It instituted the three-strikes proposal that mandates a life sentence for anyone convicted of three 'violent' felonies. The bill permitted children as young as thirteen to be tried as adult."[138]

Obama, along with Biden, and like many of their democratic predecessors, believed that it was critical to look tough on crime. Michelle Alexander pronounces, "Obama has revived President Clinton's Community Oriented Policing Services (COPS) program and increased funding for the Byrne grant program—two of the worst federal drug programs of the Clinton era.... These programs, despite their benign names, are responsible for the militarization of policing, SWAT teams, Pipeline drug task forces, and the laundry list of drug-war horrors.... Obama's budget for law enforcement is actually worse than the Bush administration's in terms of the ratio of dollars devoted to prevention and drug treatment as opposed to law enforcement."[139]

It is quite impressive for a supposedly progressive president to devote more money to law enforcement than to prevention and drug treatment, than a president known for cutting social services.

We cannot forget that during the presidency of Barack Obama, we saw racial tension erupt in Ferguson, Baltimore, New York, Chicago, and Cleveland. Although Obama should not be directly blamed for the causes of these incidents, it should be abundantly clear that he has fallen well short of the savior that many blacks hoped he would be.

The Five-O

All you need to understand is that the officer carries with him the power of the American state and the weight of an American legacy, and they necessitate that of the bodies destroyed every year, some wild and disproportionate number of them will be black. ~ Ta-Nehisi Coates

Michael Brown, Eric Garner, Tamir Rice, Freddie Gray, John Crawford III, Tony Robinson, Sandra Bland, Rekia Boyd, Amadou Diallo. What do all these names have in common? They were all black, they were all killed by police officers, they were all unarmed, and no police officer ever spent any time in jail for their killings.

No one has been in the spotlight more than the police over the last few years. As a result, they have been criticized, mocked, and even murdered. The police have been viewed with skepticism at best, and illegitimate at worst. They have been portrayed as militarized, violent, racist, and reckless. So, what should we make of this? Are these views justified and accurate?

The answer to these questions, I believe, is yes and no. Yes, there are racist police officers. No, they are not all racist. Yes, police brutality is a legitimate concern. No, not all police officers are reckless and violent. Yes, we should be critical and skeptical of the police. No, they should not be blamed for all the problems that exist in marginalized, mostly black and Hispanic neighborhoods. Yes, there needs to be more reform and accountability for law enforcement. No, police reform will not eliminate all of the racial and class problems that prevail in America.

But how has the United States become so divided between the police and people of color? Finding the answers to this question will require us to go back in time and evaluate the history of law enforcement in this country.

It is impossible for whites to truly understand the outrage felt by blacks when a police officer kills or beats an innocent African-American. What many whites may not realize is the inherent privilege of simply being white. Our white skin allows us the luxury of not being presumed guilty. The

123

wallet we may be holding will not as likely be mistaken for a gun. The toy gun we are playing with will most likely not result in a death sentence. A broken taillight will unlikely lead to the escalation of violence. A hoody and sagging pants will probably not lead to a violent assault or even an excuse for a stop. The link between the history of white vigilantism and modern police brutality against blacks is undeniable.

Wages of Rebellion puts it this way:

> African-Americans know too intimately how judicial systems work to protect white vigilantes and police who gun down unarmed black men, women, and children. There is a long, tragic continuum from the murders and lynching of blacks following Emancipation to the strangulation on July 17, 2014, of Eric Garner in Staten Island by police who charged him with selling loose, untaxed cigarettes, as well as the shooting to death on August 9, 2014, in Ferguson, Missouri, of an unarmed African-American teenager, Michael Brown, by a white police officer. It is lynching by another name. The police officers who carried out these murders, offering a window into a court system that routinely ignores black suffering and murder, were never charged with a crime. And the longer this continues the more likely become random and violent acts of retaliation, which the state will label terrorism and use to justify odious forms of repression. Once this eruption happens, as American history has illustrated, white vigilantes, along with the organs of state security, are given carte blanche to attack and even murder those who are demonized as enemies of the state"[140]

We must understand the deeply rooted tension between law enforcement and African-Americans that has existed since the founding of our nation. The injustices blacks suffered at the hands of the dominant white society began well before the modern police were established.

Before there was policing as we know it today, slave patrols served the purpose of racial control. During slavery, slave revolts were a constant and obsessive fear of whites, who were wary of any unsupervised activity by black people. Due to the ever growing concern of slave uprisings, slave codes were created in the late seventeenth century, which shifted the responsibilities of enforcement from the overseers to the entire white population. In the 1680s, the militia sent out patrols to catch runaways, prevent slave gatherings, and essentially intimidate blacks.

The whole white population was not only complicit in maintaining the status quo of slavery, but they were actively responsible for keeping blacks confined to the shackles of slavery. Slave patrols were not merely held by volunteers; many communities mandated all whites to serve on slave patrols.

Kristian Williams lists the three stages that the state used to control slave behavior. "First, legislation was passed restricting the activities of slaves. Second, this legislation was supplemented with requirements that every White man enforce its demands. Third, over time this system of enforcement gradually came to be regulated, either by the militia or by the courts."[141]

The South's preferred methods of policing were far less organized than anything that resembles policing today. Although this cannot be considered modern policing, it has similarities in that citizens served their communities to maintain law and order.

Freeing of the slaves incited a fear inside whites that was inescapable. It was precisely what they had feared for so long: blacks freely roaming, raping their women, and murdering their children. Slavery worked well as both an economic system and a system of racial control. Without slavery whites would need to implement a new system that kept blacks at the bottom.

If the local sheriff was not directly involved in a crime against an African- American, then he was complicit in allowing others to dish out vigilante justice. Sheriff's would often allow lynch mobs to take suspected criminals out of jail and lynch them. They would regularly inform the angry, white vigilantes where the alleged black criminal was located. Sometimes they would even bring the supposed perpetrator of an unforgivable crime to the lynch mob.

Sheriffs were also instrumental in creating the convict leasing and debt peonage system and were the glue that held this type of neoslavery together and allowed it to persist for so long, at the expense of many black lives.

In his book *Devil in the Grove*, Pulitzer Prize-winning author Gilbert King writes about Sheriff Willis McCall and the Groveland Four, young black men who were accused of raping a white girl in Florida in 1948. After word got out lynch mobs formed, tracked down one of the suspects, Ernest Thomas, and murdered him. Sheriff McCall and other officers who were present at the scene of the killing, claimed that the suspect had a gun and reached for it, resulting in him being killed.

The other three suspects—Charles Greenlee, Samuel Shepherd and Walter Irvin—were taken in by McCall and his goons and subjected to vicious beatings. Two of the suspects were coerced into a confession. The third suspect, Walter Irvin, refused to confess. Despite insufficient evidence, the white jury in racist Lake County, Florida, convicted all three men. Two were sentenced to death, the other to a life sentence.

Prominent NAACP lawyer and later Supreme Court Justice, Thurgood Marshall, took up the case and got it overturned. After the verdict when Sheriff McCall was transporting Shepherd and Irvin, he shot and killed Shepherd and attempted to murder Irvin, who survived by playing dead. Lake County Deputy James Yates later drove by and attempted to finish Irvin off by shooting him in the neck.

Miraculously, Irvin survived this as well, and later reported that McCall staged the scene to make it look like he and Shepherd were trying to escape. An all-white jury, made up of McCall's friends and supporters, acquitted the sheriff of all charges. Irvin was later retried and again convicted and sentenced to death. The sentence, however, was later reduced to life in prison by the governor of Florida.

This horrific story of the injustice against blacks is by no means an anomaly. Sheriffs, their deputies, lawyers, and white citizens all worked in unison to oppress African-Americans in the South.

126

As more Americans began to move to urban areas, policing began to transform. According to Kristian Williams, "As cities industrialized, White workers formed another troublesome group. Efforts to control these new dangerous classes: were more legalistic and impartial (in form, if not in application) than those directed against the slaves. Laws against vagrancy, gambling, prostitution, loitering, cursing, and drinking (The nineteenth-century equivalent of our current war on drugs) brought the habits of the poor into the jurisdiction of the police, and the police directed their suspicions accordingly."[142]

The police could now roam the streets arresting and harassing whomever they liked, based on petty offenses. Naturally, this affected blacks disproportionately. The police often enjoyed the help of the Ku Klux Klan to harass, arrest, attack, and kill blacks, communists, Jews, and other undesirables. In fact, many police officers were part of the Klan. In 1922 Los Angeles District Attorney Thomas Lee Woolwine raided the local Klan headquarters and discovered that the Los Angeles chief of police, Louis D. Oaks, Sheriff William I. Trager, and US Attorney Joseph Burke were all connected to the Klan as were dozens of other police officers, judges, and public officials throughout California.

> When the Klan was at the peak of its power in Colorado, it counted among its members many prominent businessmen, state representatives and senators, the Colorado secretary of state, four judges, two federal narcotics agents, and scores of police. In Denver, the mayor, city attorney, manager of public safety, two deputy sheriffs, the chief of police, and a police inspector were all Klan members. Former mayor George D. Begole claimed the Klan controlled the civil service commission, fire department, and police.
>
> During the 1930s, about 100 Michigan cops-including the chief of police in Pontiac-joined either the Klan or its successor organization the Black Legion.... Michael Novick of

People against Racist Terror documented more than fifty
incidents of police involvement in racist organizing between
1976 and 1994.[143]

The police have also used riots as an excuse to invoke an unnecessary
amount of violence on African-Americans. Other times, the police would refuse
to help blacks during riots. When police officers acted in these ways, they
would rarely receive any type of discipline. The violence perpetrated against
protesters during the Civil Rights Era by the police showed the world the
resistance blacks were up against. Images of blacks being beaten with clubs,
hosed by water, and bitten by police dogs became iconic during this time. Even
today the police seem to use discretion and patience more often when
attempting to de-escalate white rioters as opposed to black rioters.

Amadou Diallo, an African immigrant, was by all accounts a good and
law-abiding resident of the Bronx. Just after midnight on February 4, 1999,
Diallo was shot 19 times by four officers of New York Police Department's
Street Crimes Unit. The plain-clothed officers were riding in an unmarked
Ford Taurus when they noticed Diallo standing near his building and thought
he resembled the description of a serial rapist.

According to a witness, the police officers did not identify themselves.
Diallo began to run up the steps towards his apartment, ignoring orders to stop
and show his hands. Diallo then reached for his pocket and took out his wallet.
At this point, one of the officers yelled that he had a gun, and they started
shooting. One of the officers tripped backwards off the stairs. Thinking he may
have been shot, the other officers continued to shoot Diallo, firing a total of 41
shots. Diallo was pronounced dead, holding only his wallet.

The officers were charged with second-degree murder, depraved
indifference to human life, and reckless endangerment. A judge ordered the
trial moved from the Bronx, which is two-thirds black and Hispanic to Albany,
150 miles north and 89 percent white. All four officers were acquitted.

This tragic killing of a black man illustrates a common theme among
police killings. First, there was the racial profiling and the assumption of

danger because it was a black man. Next, there was the escalation of a potential threat, instead of the use of persuasion and de-escalation tactics. Then there was the excessive use of force, justified because a police officer's life was perceived threatened, and the later massaging of the judicial system leading to the acquittal and lack of any type of accountability for the officers involved. The fault was also put on Diallo for running from officers and not putting his hands up. But in reality, his black skin condemned him to death far before he started running.

The NYPD enforced Mayor Rudy Giuliani's stop-and-frisk policy, which targeted blacks and Latinos. No gun was retrieved in 99.9 percent of stops. Profiling was not only unsuccessful in taking guns out of the hands of criminals, but this program furthered the distrust between minorities and the police.

The police like to explain profiling as part of their job. They see profiling as a way to prevent crimes from happening. If they can identify certain statistics, behaviors, and trends, then can avoid potential threats. This is a convenient way to justify racial profiling.

Kristian Williams explains, "Employers could justify discrimination in hiring by explaining that, statistically speaking, certain groups tend to be less qualified." He continues, "The moral and political faults of such reasoning are obvious, but there is a logical fallacy as well. An individual's ability to pay the rent, to perform a job, or to obey the law, cannot be judged on the basis of statistical performance of a group to which it belongs."[144]

For example, suggesting that blacks commit robbery more than any other race based on statistical evidence can be interpreted different ways. Statistics can be used to justify that since blacks commit robberies more than any other race they need to be profiled, but another way to interpret the data is to conclude that police officers target blacks more based on their biases, and that is the reason the data shows that blacks rob more.

There has been a plethora of studies that have shown extreme racial biases in policing. Temple University's John Lamberth analyzed the data from 1995 and 1996 on traffic stops by Maryland State Police. Blacks comprised 17 percent of Maryland licensed drivers. But 72 percent of those stopped and searched were black. Half of the Maryland State Police traffic officers stopped black people in at least 80 percent of their stops. One officer stopped Blacks in 95 percent of his stops, and two officers stopped only black people. And a study in Omaha, Nebraska, in 2011 found blacks were almost three times as likely to be searched as whites during traffic stops.

Similar trends have been found in cities throughout the United States. Williams concludes, "The studies show that people of color are more likely than White people to be pulled over, removed from the car, and searched. But they reveal something else as well: race is useless as an indicator of criminality. While blacks and Latinos accounted for 78 percent of those searched at the south end of the New Jersey Turnpike during the year 2000, evidence was more reliably found by searching white people: 25 percent of white people searched had contraband, as compared to 13 percent of black people and 5 percent of Latinos."[145]

After racially profiling Diallo and presuming his guilt by the color of his skin, the officers of the Street Crimes Unit reportedly took out their guns and started moving aggressively towards Diallo. Put yourself in Diallo's shoes: here he was alone late at night, minding his own business, when four large men in civilian clothing approached him with guns blazing. Frightened, Diallo did what any rational human being would do in this situation. He ran. After he ran, the events quickly escalated, ending in tragedy.

If the officers had approached Diallo in a less threatening way, the outcome may have been very different. It seems that in many situations, the first instinct of many police officers are to use or threaten to use force. Tamir Rice was shot and killed by police officer Timothy Loehmann within seconds after he and his partner encountered him at a playground where Rice was playing with a toy gun.

The reasons for the quick use of force by officers vary. Officers may be quick to use force because that is how they are trained. It may be as a result of the dangers of their job and our heavily armed society. It also may have to do with their conscious and subconscious biases of black criminality. Whatever the reasons, the use of force should be the last option, not the first.

After the NYPD officers escalated the situation, excessive force was on full display. They fired 41 shots in the matter of seconds. The officers claim that their lives were in danger, and their belief that one of their officers was shot, led to the violent assault on Diallo. The rhetoric of officers being in danger is a convenient justification for many shootings. It is a virtual get out of jail free card, or more appropriately a never go to jail or even be indicted card. After shooting a civilian, officers can assert that they acted in self-defense, and because the system is weighed heavily in their favor, this excuse typically exonerates them of any criminal charges.

Police and their sympathizers will often blame the victim after a police killing. Just like it was Diallo's "fault" for running away and not stopping and putting his hands where the officers could see them upon command. It was Sandra Bland's fault for talking back to Texas State Trooper Brian Encinia. Walter Scott should have never run away from North Carolina officer Michael Slager. Michael Brown shouldn't have been walking in the middle of the street. Freddy Gray should have never made eye contact with Baltimore police officers. Tamir Rice should not have been playing with a toy gun. Eric Garner should not have been selling cigarettes. Alton Sterling should not have been selling CDs.

We forget that these seemingly innocent mistakes, if we want to even call them mistakes, have proved to be death sentences for African-Americans. We neglect to realize that simply based on the color of our skin, we are either subjected, or not subjected, to police brutality.

As I was volunteering at the Better Boys Foundation (BBF), located on Chicago's predominately black West Side, I tuned into a conversation that an adult was having with kids who are part of the BBF program.

She asked, "What did Laquan do wrong?" referring to Laquan McDonald who was shot 16 times and killed unprovoked by Chicago police officer Jason Van Dyke.

The kids all answered: *He should have stayed home like his mom asked him to*, as if they had rehearsed the answer many times. Although this was good advice, I found it sad because it's a harsh reality that black kids and

131

adults alike have to take extra precaution when going about their daily routine. Black parents have to talk to their kids and explain how to act in order to lessen the chances of being victimized by the police.

Many black drivers know to put their license and registration on the dash of their car prior to being approached by a police officer, so it does not look like they are reaching for a gun when asked for their license and registration. This is how Philando Castile was shot and killed in Minnesota.

As a child, my parents never had to have a talk with me to explain how to act around police. I never thought about being harassed or abused by the police growing up. It's a privilege I didn't even know I had. It is a privilege that all white people have, especially those who live in affluent and upscale neighborhoods. I never had to worry that the color of my skin would make me a potential target for police brutality. This, unfortunately, is a privilege that blacks do not have.

After the killing of a black person by the police, the public is often critical of the ensuing riots or protests. In the wake of Michael Brown's death by officer Darren Wilson and then the failure to indict him, riots broke out. Riots were condemned by all, and the public seemed baffled that blacks would act in such a reckless manner over a single police killing. What is generally misunderstood is the palpable tension leading up to these events. The killing of Michael Brown was simply the tipping point, the straw that broke the camel's back.

After the riots, the Department of Justice's investigation of the Ferguson Police Department proved what blacks who lived in Ferguson already knew. The report showed racism, racial profiling, and a pattern to generate revenue through ticketing a disproportionate number of African-Americans. The tension that had built up over years between the Ferguson Police Department and black members of the community simply came to a breaking point when the unarmed Michael Brown was killed and left to rot in the street for four hours.

The beating of Rodney King by Los Angeles police officers and the riots that erupted soon after show similarities to other acts of police brutality. After a 10-minute car chase, LAPD officers ordered the unarmed King out of his car, tased him, and then began brutally beating him. The encounter was caught on tape, showing three officers taking turns beating King—clubbing him fifty-six times, kicking him in the body and head—while other officers looked on, including Sergeant Stacey Koon.

Nothing about this was unusual, except for the fact that it was caught on camera and then played for the whole world to see. The Rodney King beating had similarities to the Diallo killing in that the indicted officers in both incidents were tried in predominately white areas where they would receive much sympathy.

The site of the trial against the LAPD officers took place in Simi Valley, located in predominantly white Ventura County, where many police officers lived in communities known for strong law and order attitudes.

Similar to the riots that took place in St. Louis after Officer Wilson was not charged for shooting Michael Brown, Los Angeles erupted in rage after the acquittal of all officers involved in the Rodney King beating. Like in Ferguson, the South Central neighborhood of Los Angeles, was plagued with police abuse, with 2,500 excessive force complaints against the LAPD. The racial strain was evident for years between the LAPD and the poor, mostly black and Latino residents. Once again, the Rodney King beating and the lack of accountability for the perpetrators, created the perfect storm.

Also similar to the Ferguson riots were the way black protesters and rioters were portrayed by the media and the public. The media painted images of black rage and criminality. The media was also misleading by focusing on violence committed against whites and Korean merchants. But only 10 percent of arrests were for violent crime. The unfair depiction of blacks not only blames the victim and encourages racism, but takes the emphasis off the root problem: police brutality.

Cities only occasionally erupt in rage after witnessing an act of police brutality, but often explode in anger after the failure to bring police officers to justice. This happened both in the Rodney King beating and the killing of Michael Brown. On Democracynow! Cornel West said, "Justice and accountability are necessary to ending tension over killings by police."

By allowing police officers to kill and face no consequences, we are putting salt on an open wound. We are saying that the police are above the law that they are supposed to uphold. We are condoning this type of behavior and allowing it to persist. According to the *Washington Post* there have been thousands of police killings, but only 54 officers charged over the last decade.[146]

If we have any hope of lessening the divide between blacks and the police, more accountability for police actions is a good place to start.

#

On a late March night in 2012, a group of four African-Americans were walking in the dangerous and gang infested West Side neighborhood of North Lawndale, when a car pulled up to them. An argument ensued, gunshots were fired, and a 22-year-old woman lay dying from a gunshot wound to the back of her head. If you were envisioning a gang-related, drive-by shooting you were wrong. The shooter was not a member of the Gangster Disciples or the Vice Lords, but another organization known for their history of violence and brutality: the Chicago Police Department.

Dante Servin, a veteran detective of the CPD, was off duty and in his personal car when he confronted a group of African-Americans he believed were talking too loudly. They started arguing. Then Servin claimed that Antonio Cross took out something that Servin mistook for a gun, and Servin then fired multiple shots from his car at the group. One of the bullets hit Antonio Cross in the hand and another mortally wounded Rekia Boyd. The object that Servin allegedly mistook for a gun was a cell phone. The only armed person was Dante Servin.

Family and friends of Rekia Boyd fought for the indictment of Dante Servin, and former state's attorney Anita Alvarez inexplicably charged him with involuntary manslaughter, making Servin the first CPD officer to stand trial in 15 years. Servin was eventually acquitted of charges as the judge found Servin's actions beyond reckless and thus not appropriate for the charges he was being tried for. So Servin walked out of court a free man and continued his work in the CPD.

Later, the Chicago Police Department's then superintendent, Garry McCarthy, was under much scrutiny after the killing of Laquan McDonald, prompting him to pursue the firing of Dante Servin, almost four years after the shooting death of Rekia Boyd. But before he could be fired, Servin was allowed to resign enabling him to keep his pension.

This story, although unique in some ways, is not so atypical considering the history of the Chicago Police Department. The CPD has long been known for its corruption, torture, and violence. Corruption was routine in Al Capone's heyday. More than one hundred people—mostly African-American men—accused Jon Burge of torturing them through electric shocks, beating, and suffocation into confessing. The true number of victims under the former CPS commander is most likely much higher. And recently, reports from *The Guardian* have indicated that the CPD have used a building that many refer to as a black site, to house mostly black suspects without any legal representation.

Police misconduct of blacks and Latinos are not uncommon in Chicago. As the Black Panthers expanded and instilled fear in the United States government, they were hunted down by the FBI and other organizations. Perhaps one of the most infamous attacks occurred in Chicago. Fred Hampton, the chairman of the Illinois chapter of the Black Panther Party was living on the West Side of Chicago, when in 1969 police armed with submachine guns shot their way into Hampton's apartment, firing ninety-eight rounds and, killing Fred Hampton and Mark Clark, head of the Peoria, Illinois, Panthers. Clark fired a single round of return fire. Hampton was shot three times in the chest and twice in the head.

The police defended their actions by claiming that they had been "viciously" attacked, but the evidence contradicted their statements. Eventually, after a long-fought civil rights lawsuit, family members were awarded a $1.85 million settlement. No officers were ever charged for any wrongdoing.

The trend of violence and misconduct towards blacks and the subsequent lack of accountability for the CPD has continued according to Sarah Macaraeg and Alison Flowers in *Who Do You Serve, Who Do You Protect?*

At least 21 CPD officers are currently serving on the force, some with honors, after shooting citizens under highly questionable circumstances, resulting in at least $30.2 million in taxpayer-funded City of Chicago settlements thus far.

Six officers who have shot and killed civilians also have a large volume of unpenalized complaints of misconduct.

At least 500 CPD officers with more than 10 misconduct complaints over a five-year period (2001-2006) are still serving on the force. Their combined salary is $42.5 million dollars.

Four lieutenants, the director and an organizer of the Chicago Alternative Policing Strategy (CAPS), 55 detectives, a field training officer, and 69 sergeants are among the 500 CPD officers with more than 10 misconduct complaints over the five- year period.

Police officer Raymond Piwnicki, now a detective, had the highest number of complaints in the five-year period, with 55 misconduct complaints and zero penalties. Piwnicki was awarded the Superintendent's Award of Valor in 2013-for a shooting as a result of which he is now a defendant in a civil suit that cites his "deliberate indifference" to a fellow officer's deadly force.

More than 60 of the 662 police officers with at least 10 misconduct complaints hailed from the Special Operations Section, which was responsible for 1,311 complaints in these five years of data alone.

They continue:

From 2002 to 2008, out of 90 excessive force complaints specifically denoting improper "Weapon, use-display of," all but eight were dismissed, with only five noting the violation. During this time period, a paralyzed man, Cornelius Ware, was shot and killed by officer Anthony Blake,

136

whose record noted a weapon complaint as "unfounded." The City of Chicago later awarded Ware's family a settlement of $5.25 million.

During the 2001 to 2006 span, more than three dozen police officers had 29 or more misconduct complaints on their records, more than double the number of complaints accumulated by indicted Chicago police commander Glenn Evans during the same period.[147]

The majority of the victims of this abuse are blacks and other minorities. The Chicago organization We Charge Genocide reports that more than 75 percent of those shot by Chicago police from 2009 to 2013 were black. We cannot continue to ignore the injustices that are transpiring in our most vulnerable neighborhoods by the people that are supposed to protect them.

As I was driving through Austin on a hot summer evening, I stopped at a red light and noticed a struggle between a black male and three police officers. I am uncertain of what led to the confrontation, but I watched as the officers tried to apprehend the man who was resisting tenaciously. Was he resisting because he did not want to get caught or because he was afraid of what the police might do to him? Blacks justifiably must feel a strong sense of fear when they are confronted by cops. No wonder so many run like Amadou Diallo did.

As I was watching the police officers try to apprehend the man, people started coming from all directions with their cell phones out, taking videos of the scuffle. I wondered: *Were they capturing the next viral video of another black man being killed by police?*

The officers eventually subdued the stubborn man. They did not use excessive force and maintained their cool despite a tough situation. I thought to myself, how hard it must be to deal with situations similar to this on a regular basis. I considered how strenuous it must be for police officers that work in violent areas to be calm under pressure, when they know many residents in these communities are armed and dangerous. I contemplated how difficult it must be to deal with society's most desperate and dangerous offenders and not start to think less of them and everyone else in their community.

Yet, I also thought of the lack of trust black communities like Austin have in the police to feel the need to record every potential tragedy. How little faith many residents have that officers will act honorably and that the only possible justice that a victim of police violence can hope for is in the form of a video that clearly shows wrongdoing. And even then, there is still a good chance that justice will not be served.

If we have any hope of creating safer and more just communities, we will have to bridge the divide between the police and the communities they serve.

Mythbusting

Nothing in the world is more dangerous than sincere ignorance and conscientious stupidity. ~ *Martin Luther King, Jr*

Martin Luther King, Jr. warned us about ignorance. He understood how dangerous it can be. He saw ignorance every day. I also see the danger of ignorance, and I see it displayed by people far too often. African-Americans have been the victims of ignorance from the time they arrived in the United States and still are today. I know, because I was once ignorant of what I did not know. Now I will attempt to dismiss myths about African-Americans that have persisted for far too long.

I would first like to point out that any stereotyping or generalizing is inaccurate, hurtful, and racist. The late Elie Wiesel, a holocaust survivor and the author of the book *Night*, said, "No human race is superior; no religious faith is inferior. All collective judgments are wrong. Only racists make them."

By judging a whole race of people, you are condemning them all guilty of whatever your preconceived views of them are. I believe that most people understand that these kinds of judgments are wrong and hurtful, but I am not sure they completely understand the consequences racism can produce. The most extreme example of this is the Holocaust. Jews were persecuted, humiliated, and murdered at rates that are truly unfathomable. We all know that Hitler was a man of unsurpassable evil, but what we also need to realize is the extreme hate and prejudice that most Germans and other Europeans felt for Jews. The indifference and fear felt by millions of people around the world permitted the extermination of millions of Jews. The Holocaust, although an extraordinary example, was far from the only time in history that a group of people were persecuted because of their religion or race.

The United States deceived, removed, and murdered millions of Native Americans in order to occupy their land. We did this in the name of patriotism. We justified this by believing that Native Americans were savages and considered them less than human.

Yet another example of genocide resulting in the dehumanization of a group of people is the mass murder of Tutsis and Hutu moderates at the hands of the Hutu majority in Rwanda. The Tutsis and the Hutus are almost indistinguishable in appearance, but as Germany and Belgium ruled Rwanda, they determined that the Tutsis looked more Caucasian and therefore designated them as the ruling class. This caste system led to hate and eventually violence between the Tutsis and the Hutus. The worst of the violence occurred in 1994, when the Hutu majority massacred well over 500,000 Tutsis in a 100-day period.

There are countless examples of violence and hate that were the result of one group of people thinking they were superior to another group. This is precisely why we need to be conscious of the harm our racist notions can cause. We also need to educate ourselves and our kids on the falsehood of racist myths and replace them with the truth.

The origin of most racist stereotypes of African-Americans can be traced back to slavery. Most Southern whites believed blacks were inferior. They also believed that African-Americans could not handle freedom or care for themselves and were best suited for a life in slavery. Like the Nazi beliefs that the Aryan race of white skin, blue eyes, and blond hair was superior, whites believed that any physical features that differed from whites were inferior.

There was also a widespread belief that blacks were less intelligent than whites, validated by questionable studies conducted to "prove" what most people already believed: that blacks were inherently less intelligent than whites. In 1839, Samuel George Morton determined that Caucasians had the largest skulls, and therefore the largest brains, and blacks the smallest. His tests were the forerunner of phrenology, which sought to determine character and intelligence by interpreting the shape of the skull.

Racist stereotypes were also perpetuated by minstrel shows, theatrical productions where white performers painted their faces black—also known as Blackface—and later by blacks who portrayed stereotypical black behavior in front of an audience. One of the most famous characters was Jim Crow, and is where the term Jim Crow originated from. Other characters were Zip Coon, Mammy, Buck, Uncle Tom, Wench, and Pickaninny. These characters depicted common stereotypes that blacks were lazy, oversexed, and dumb. Sadly, many of these stereotypes that originated in the mid-1800s still persist.

Today it's rare for someone to openly claim blacks are inherently less intelligent than others. Politicians know it would be political suicide to state such blatant racism. Likewise, most people are aware that it would be social suicide to endorse these same ideas. However, these feelings of black inferiority still exist today, just on a subtler level. It's not uncommon for people to criticize how blacks talk. People will think or say things like, "Learn how to speak English."

Black vernacular is associated with a lack of intelligence by many but in *American Apartheid*, Massey and Denton explain that linguists have shown black language "is by no means a degenerate, or illogical version of Standard American English; rather, it constitutes a complex, rich, and expressive language on its own right, with a consistent grammar, pronunciation, and lexicon all its own ... [that] evolved independently from Standard American English because blacks were historically separated from whites by caste, class, and region; but among the most powerful influences on black speech has been the residential segregation that black have experienced since early in the century."[148]

I have found it quite impressive that blacks can transfer from street talk to a more traditional English and back almost like they are bilingual. It is not at all surprising that blacks have developed their own language, when considering the isolation they have lived in. Knowing that black ghettos were created by a system of segregation and isolation, it is quite perplexing to now criticize blacks for developing their own culture and language.

Blacks have always been stereotyped simply by the color of their skin. There has been a significant amount of further research that has shown that the darker someone's skin is, the more they get discriminated against. Studies show that Puerto Ricans, who are typically darker than Mexicans, get discriminated against more than Mexicans. Conversely, several sociological and anthropological studies have uncovered strong correlations between lighter skin and higher earnings and between thinner noses and lips and higher socioeconomic status.

To say that skin color and even the pigment of the skin is the only factor to determine discrimination would be inaccurate. Class is another factor that plays a role in how a black American is perceived. An African-American who looks and acts more white is less likely to be judged. For example, a dark- skinned, black male in his late teens who wears saggy pants and talks ghetto is more likely to be labeled a criminal, regardless of his character or reputation. Now it's true that everyone is judged based on their appearance to a certain degree, but being black exacerbates this issue because blacks have to deal with the stereotypes of being black, in addition to the judgments of appearance. Low income blacks, who are isolated in predominately black ghettos, have developed their own unique culture. But because this culture is generally not accepted outside of the ghetto, many blacks are subjected to false stereotypes and prejudices.

Another stereotype is that blacks are lazy, which is how they were presented in minstrel shows. It's quite baffling that white slave holders, who forced black slaves to do all their work for free, considered blacks to be lazy and incompetent. But then again, there is much in today's society that screams of hypocrisy. It is also bewildering that blacks today, are still considered lazy by some. It's not uncommon to hear politicians or the media rambling on about how welfare recipients are all lazy people who don't try to get a job and only want to live off the government. And when politicians speak in this kind of encrypted language, they are typically referring to African-Americans.

The demonization of welfare recipients took full force under President Ronald Reagan in the '80s. While campaigning, Reagan described a "welfare queen" that lived in the South Side of Chicago who "has eighty names, thirty addresses, twelve Social Security cards and is collecting veteran's benefits on four non-existing deceased husbands. And she is collecting Social Security on her cards. She's got Medicaid, getting food stamps, and she is collecting welfare under each of her names. Her tax-free cash income is over $150,000."[149]

When crack hit the streets in 1985, Reagan and the media used stories of crack babies and crack whores to scare the public into supporting the war on drugs. Although Reagan never blatantly connected crack to blacks, everyone knew who he was referring to as he bashed mothers who produced babies that were supposedly addicted to crack. The public was consumed by the media's coverage of the crack epidemic and soon enough, crack became synonymous with black inner city Americans.

Reagan's full on assault on welfare and the poor was quite impressive. He paid for building the military by cutting social services. Reagan was not the only one. Both Bush's and Bill Clinton also significantly defunded social programs. Today the stigma of welfare recipients has not changed much. Many people, especially Republicans, don't want their money going to people they perceive as too lazy to find a job. We never have enough money to spend on people that need it the most, but we don't mind spending money to fund wars that supposedly make us safer and on corporate tax subsidies that go to wealthy corporations.

According to Howard Zinn:

> Democrats often joined Republicans in denouncing welfare programs. Presumably, this was done to gain political support from a middle-class public that believed they were paying taxes to support teenage mothers and people they thought too lazy to work. Much of the public did not know, and were not informed by either political leaders or the media, that welfare took a tiny part of the taxes, and military spending took a huge chunk of it.

A New York Times/CBS News poll conducted in early 1992 showed that public opinion on welfare changed depending on how the question was worded. If the word 'welfare' was used, 44 percent of those questioned said too much was being spent on welfare (while 50 percent either that the right amount was being spent, or that too little was being spent. But when the question was about "assistance to the poor," only 13 percent thought too much was being spent, and 64 percent thought too little was being spent.[150]

In 2012 the average American taxpayer making $50,000 per year paid just $36 towards the food stamps program and just six more dollars for the rest of the America's social safety net programs. It seems as if the government and media have influenced our views on how the word welfare is interpreted.

I have had people tell me that they considered blacks to be dirty. I thought to myself: *What do you mean dirty? Do you mean they roll in mud like pigs? Or that blacks don't shower often?* I was confused. I knew that calling someone dirty is a way of saying that they are lower than you, but how and why are blacks considered dirty to some people?

In the Pulitzer Prize-winning book, *Arab and Jew*, David Shipler discusses the bitter and never-ending conflicts between Jews and Arabs. He analyzes the deeply embedded stereotypes that Israeli Jews have of Arabs living in or around Israel and vice versa. After reading this book, I noticed that many Israeli Jews had or have similar prejudices and stereotypes of the marginalized Arabs living amongst them as white Americans have or had regarding blacks. The stereotype of the violent Arab is also very common. This book was written almost thirty years ago, so I'm unaware if the same stereotypes still apply today. Nonetheless, it's interesting that on a different continent and in a different culture, many of the same stereotypes blacks have been associated with by the dominant and oppressive white majority, have also been associated with Arabs by a similar ruling class of Israeli Jews in the

Middle East.

It has also occurred to me that the dirty label given to many black Americans may have stemmed from the stereotype that blacks were disease ridden. During the antebellum slavery era, physicians believed that blacks were carriers of various diseases such as syphilis, which threatened the health of whites. It was a common belief amongst physicians that syphilis affected blacks differently than whites because blacks had a less evolved nervous systems.

In Medical Apartheid Harriet Washington writes that most physicians also believed "diseases manifested differently in blacks, and that blacks could not be trusted to take medicine, follow treatment, or maintain basic standards of hygiene without white supervision."[151]

This not only "proved" blacks were dirty and disease ridden but, once again, justified the myth that blacks natural state was slavery. For example, some physicians presumed that blacks were immune to overheating and malaria. This rationale led to yet another justification that blacks were innately predisposed to the conditions of slavery.

Another stereotype that had deeply rooted origins and still exists today is that blacks are oversexed, which also dates back to the antebellum South. Slaves were often sold for more money if they were attractive. In addition, slave masters paid more for women's reproductive ability so they would birth babies who would then become slaves themselves, enabling slave owners to increase their profits. It is estimated one of every five black women of childbearing age gave birth.

Washington says females were often raped and forced into sexual relationships. "Girls were forced or enticed into sexual relationships at an unhealthily early age by owners who cited the girls' supposedly hot-blooded African nature.... Whites ascribed black women's sexual availability not to their powerlessness but to a key tenet of scientific racism: Blacks were unable to control their powerful sexual drives, which were frequently compared to those of rutting animals.... Most scientists agreed that the hot, damp tropical climate [created] a licentiousness and sexual profligacy in African women that was unknown among European women."[152]

Physical and medical examinations of slaves being purchased were a cross between sexual harassment and full on rape. Today, it's not uncommon for people to comment on how big black men's penises are (although not one of the most demeaning stereotypes, it is nonetheless untrue), or that black women are sexually lax. Once again, it is discouraging that stereotypes that were generated during slavery and bear no truth are still accepted today.

Unlike other brazenly false stereotypes of African-Americans, black criminality is more complex. Anyone who follows the news, can easily point to the fact that there are a high number of shootings in many poor, inner-city, black neighborhoods. However, to generalize and condemn all blacks with some sort of inborn trait of violence is wrong and inaccurate. Yet this is precisely the problem with generalizations and stereotypes. It is easy to say that blacks are more violent than other races in America. What is not so easy is to understand how this evolved. Khalil Gibran Muhammad, the author of *The Condemnation of Blackness*, traces the idea of black criminality back to its roots.

Using new data from the 1870, 1880, and 1890 U.S. census reports, the earliest demographic studies to measure the full scale of black life in freedom, these post-emancipation writers helped to create the racial knowledge necessary to shape the future of race relations. Racial knowledge that had been dominated by anecdotal, hereditarian, and pseudo-scientific theories or face and society and new tools of analysis, namely racial statistics and social surveys. Out of the new methods and data sources, black criminality would emerge, alongside disease and intelligence, as a fundamental measure of black inferiority. From the 1890s through the first four decades of the twentieth century, black criminality would become one of the most commonly cited and longest-lasting justifications for black inequality and mortality in the modern urban world.[153]

Scientists and writers alike went out to prove that blacks committed more crimes because they were a fundamentally inferior race. In fact, they were very persuasive in their attempt to prove blacks were prone to criminal activity. Most of the public believed what they read, which became proof of what they already assumed. The problem with this new data, was that it did not take into consideration the many factors that led to black crime.

As discussed in earlier chapters, blacks entered the free world with nothing. They were discriminated against in almost every way, making it difficult to obtain a job that provided the finances essential to living. They were victims of vigilante and police violence. Blacks had little protection and were presented few opportunities to succeed. In an effort to flee terror and make a better life for themselves, they migrated to the urban North. In the North, they were met with more violence and discrimination. They were systematically segregated into poor ghettos. The poor ghettos of the North gave them few resources to succeed. With little hope, drugs and violence became a harsh reality in most inner cities. To not take the multitude of injustices blacks faced into consideration when evaluating black crime today and in the past is like not understanding that smoking cigarettes can be a precursor to lung cancer.

Shipler explains, "Scientifically, if they wanted to compare so-called genetic differences between blacks and whites, then they would have to take a group of white people who had similar experiences to black Americans. That is, they would have to find a group of white people that experienced 250 years of slavery, 100 years of Jim Crow segregation, and then let's compare our IQs."[154]

Another issue that continues today, but originated in the 1890s as black crime started to increase, is how law enforcement and the general public reacted to black crime. Muhammad notes, "White criminality was society's problem, but black criminality was black people's problem. Such thinking contributed to discriminatory social work approaches and crime-fighting policies in black communities, with devastating consequences, including the worsening of social conditions. Among whites, struggling neighborhoods were considered a cause of crime and a reason to intervene. Among blacks, they

147

were considered a sign of pathology and a reason for neglect."[155]

This massive problem shaped black criminality 100 years ago and continues to this day. Today, we still view blacks as criminals, especially young black men with sagging pants and tattoos. And when blacks do commit crimes, we condemn the whole race, while whites who commit crimes are judged on an individual basis.

When we condemn a whole race based on the actions of only a few, we create stereotypes, and racism flourishes. The assumption that young black men are dangerous has allowed us to view them with fear, and this fear has led to the deaths of many innocent black civilians at the hands of the police.

Social Darwinism has long been a justification for racial superiority as well as class privilege. The privileged believe they have achieved their status due to hard work, and those who are less fortunate are undeserving, because they have not tried hard enough. It is a justification that on one end the privileged are deserving of their status because they have earned it, and on the other end they bear no responsibility to help those who are less fortunate because they are supposedly weaker.

Social Darwinism is a theory that gained popularity in the late nineteenth century. It is essentially the belief in survival of the fittest. In other words, the strong keep getting stronger, and the weak keep getting weaker, based on their biological traits. What many people do not realize is that Charles Darwin, the famous naturalist and geologist, did not even come up with the term survival of the fittest nor did he believe that one race was superior to another.

In his book *At the Hands of Persons Unknown*, Philip Dray explains, "Social Darwinism was unfair to its namesake. Darwin wrote of natural selection, the adaptation of an organism to its environment, and pointedly avoided equating evolution with progress or drawing other social and political conclusions from his own thesis; it was a fellow Briton, philosopher Herbert Spencer, who applied Darwin's ideas about adaptation to the survival of particular species as opposed to others and hypothesized that a struggle for survival in which the strongest wins is natural and immutable-the concept that became known as the survival of the fittest."[156]

Oddly enough, Social Darwinism has been molded into a theory that justified racism, imperialism, and eugenics by philosophers that have taken Darwin's beliefs completely out of context.

Today, when we discuss why African-Americans as a class still struggle with poverty, violence, and many other quality of life issues, it is more convenient to justify their struggles by Social Darwinism. Surely slavery, Jim Crow, lynching, housing discrimination, and so on, have nothing to do with the predicament that black Americans have found themselves in.

Indeed, it is much easier to ignore the legacies of racism in this country and justify African-Americans' inability to rise to the top by the myth of Social Darwinism. James Loewen describes this phenomenon in Sundown Towns. He explains how Americans justified reintroducing discriminatory Jim Crow laws after Reconstruction.

> The easiest way would be to declare that African-Americans had never deserved equal rights in the first place. After all, went this line of thought, conditions had significantly improved for African-Americans. Slavery was over. Now a new generation of African-Americans had come of age, never tainted by the 'peculiar institution.' Why were they still at the bottom? African-Americans themselves must be the problem. They must not work hard enough, think as well, or have as much drive, compared to whites. The Reconstruction amendments (thirteenth, fourteenth, and fifteenth) provided African- Americans with a roughly equal footing in America, most whites felt. If they were still at the bottom, it must be their own fault."[157]

How often do we blame someone else for something that went wrong in our lives? And why is it so hard to admit our own flaws and mistakes? I suppose, because it is much easier to shift the blame from ourselves. That way we don't have to endure the task of rectifying a difficult situation. We can simply avoid any guilt or responsibility by putting the focus of the blame on the victims. And African-Americans have always been an easy target to rest our collective blame on.

This kind of mindset may be less extreme and prevalent now than it used to be, but it is still the mentality of many. In fact, many Republicans and some Democrats justify their lack of empathy towards poor, marginalized groups by this logic.

Why should we support people that are too lazy or incompetent to get a job?

Why should they receive handouts that take away from my hard-earned money?

They believe that if you are struggling financially, it is most likely because you are not trying hard enough. This way of thinking is harmful and dangerous. It is not only a total lack of empathy and compassion, but it eludes reality. It denies the inescapable and sometimes insurmountable barriers that poor and marginalized groups have to overcome. Understanding that this type of perspective was formed from lies and half-truths should help us come to the realization that we need to change our frame of mind to something that resembles acceptance and compassion for all people. We don't need to justify our fallacies by inaction and more delusions; we need to come to grip with the fact that people at the bottom are not there by their own faults and may require assistance to rise out of their pit.

Stereotypes and prejudices have helped shape discriminatory laws and practices. These practices have led to the mass injustices, which have affected so many lives. If we continue to believe and vocalize these untrue and hurtful prejudices, we cannot move forward. We will be stuck in a society that turns a blind eye to the injustice that currently persists all over the country but is primarily concentrated in poor communities of color. We will continue to see streets like Austin Boulevard that divide black from white, poor from rich, and the privileged from the unprivileged.

If we continuously justify discriminatory practices because we believe in the prejudices that are motivating these practices, the problems will only deepen. It is critical that we erase our preconceived notions and replace them with the truth. Only then, can we comprehend the necessity for change. And to bring change, we need to look hard at the roots of the pre-existing problems and come up with long-lasting, powerful transformation.

Solutions

While there is a lower class, I am in it, while there is a criminal element, I am of it, and while there is a soul in prison, I am not free. ~ Eugene V. Debs

Stating problems without solutions, would be like finding the cause of cancer and not looking for the cure. Throughout this book I have demonstrated many problems that African-Americans had and are currently facing. Blacks have persevered through slavery, convict leasing, lynching, and Jim Crow laws, just to name a few. Currently, black Americans are subjected to what Michelle Alexander calls the New Jim Crow that consists of discriminatory practices that have led to the mass incarceration of Americans, affecting African-Americans disproportionately.

Before we dive into possible solutions that can help alleviate problems blacks and other minorities face, let's discuss the importance of having multiple solutions, instead of merely focusing on one.

I have found that many experts are very knowledgeable about one or two specific things. For instance, a person may be an expert on law enforcement reform. They may have studied the topic thoroughly and know it in and out.

However, they may be so focused into their area of expertise that they do not take into account all of the other variables. Solid law enforcement reform can and has helped reduce crime. Still, poverty, unemployment, parenting, education, mental illness, drugs, availability to acquire weapons, gangs, racism, discrimination, and many other factors influence crime. Therefore, a comprehensive approach to finding solutions for the problems that African-Americans encounter is essential.

The solutions that I have come up with are by no means new or groundbreaking. I will take solutions that I have studied by brilliant authors and reformers, and mold them into a comprehensive list of antidotes that I believe can alleviate many of the current issues we face.

First, we need to educate ourselves and the public on the history of racial discrimination. Second, some form of reparations need to be paid to African- Americans affected by the legacy of racism in the United States. Third, the war on drugs needs to end, and we need to find alternatives to mass incarceration.

Fourth, significant law enforcement reform is necessary. Fifth, economic inequality has to be reduced substantially. Sixth, neighborhoods need to be more integrated. Lastly, the public needs to fight for justice and equality.

As a teacher I obviously value education. I value true education that forces people to think critically. I know the importance of educating people on topics that are not well known and may be perceived controversial. Bryan Stevenson, the founder of the Equal Justice Initiative and author of the incredibly revealing book *Just Mercy*, are currently doing exactly this. They are bringing awareness to the public regarding the history of racial injustice by creating calendars, timelines, videos, reports, and a variety of other educational materials "that explore the legacy of racial bias in the United States and its continuing impact on contemporary policies and practices.... many of today's issues have been shaped by America's racial history—the history of racial injustice in particular. The legacy of slavery, racial terror, and legally supported abuse of racial minorities is not well understood. EJI believes that a deeper understanding about our nation's history of racial injustice is important to addressing contemporary questions of social justice and equality."[158]

If we do not understand the abundant injustices that African-Americans have suffered from in America, we cannot understand the current situation we are in. If we do not recognize the history of racial oppression against blacks, we cannot understand why Austin is predominantly black, crime ridden, and poor, and why Oak Park is a predominantly affluent, white neighborhood with very little crime. This is why the greater white community is baffled when primarily black cities like Ferguson and Baltimore erupt in riots after an unarmed black is killed by the police.

This is also why we have campaigns like White Lives Matter or All Lives Matter opposing the activist group Black Lives Matter. We feel that it is unjust that we have a slogan that claims that Black Lives Matter and we don't understand that black and white activists are bringing awareness to the fact that blacks are being killed at alarming rates by the police and have been for years. We can't fully grasp that groups similar to Black Lives Matter are trying to bring change to a race that has been discriminated and terrorized for centuries like no other group in the history of America (although Native Americans were forcibly moved and murdered at astonishing rates too).

When Dylann Roof massacred nine African-Americans at Emanuel African Methodist Episcopal Church in Charleston, North Carolina, controversy regarding the legitimacy of the Confederate flag incited. Government officials and the public were protesting the right that states should not be able to fly the Confederate flag over government buildings. Those opposed to the Confederate flag, suggested it was a symbol of racism and hate. Those supporting the Confederate flag advocated that it was a symbol of Southern heritage and history. It is true that the Confederate flag is a part of our history. Therefore, it is acceptable to show the Confederate flag in history museums.

However, it is a complete slap in the face to all black Americans who have to witness the flying of a flag that promotes hate and racism in public places. The Confederate flag stands for more than the history of the Civil War and the Confederate soldiers that fought in it. The flag is waved high and proud at Ku Klux Klan rallies. The flag is hung proud in the vehicles of people who still believe in white supremacy. Confederate soldiers held the Confederate flag with honor as they fought to the death to uphold the enslavement of blacks. Today, the flag is a symbol that our society is still far from the belief that African-Americans are our equals.

Yet the Confederate flag is only one small symbol of the fact that we have a long way to go in our fight for racial equality. Across the United States, but mostly in the South, there are schools, roads, monuments, landmarks, and memorials honoring former Confederate soldiers, leaders, and KKK members. Confederate Memorial Day is a national holiday in the South. Prior to 2000, Lee- Jackson-King Day was a combined national holiday in Virginia. Today,

Lee- Jackson Day and Martin Luther King Day are two separate holidays. I guess Virginia finally came to the conclusion that these three men differed slightly in their political philosophies.

In an interview by Corey Johnson of the Marshall Project, Bryan Stevenson said, "In some counties [in the South], you can't go 100 meters without seeing a marker or a stone or something that honors some Confederate general or postmaster or nurse or hospital or teacher, and yet we don't talk about slavery at all. Montgomery has 59 markers and monuments to the Confederacy, most of our streets are named after Confederate soldiers. The two largest public high schools are Robert E. Lee High and Jefferson Davis High— those are 90 percent black. And yet until a couple of years ago, there wasn't a word about slavery. Not one word."[159]

If you live in North Carolina, you may attend Charles B. Aycock High School, named after the former North Carolina Governor, a white supremacist who was responsible for imposing Jim Crow Laws. Perhaps you're a regular golfer at Wade Hampton Golf Club in North Carolina, named after a Confederate Cavalry leader who started an organization named the Red Shirts, who were responsible for massacring black voters during Reconstruction. Or maybe you are a member of the Forrest School Marching Band located in Tennessee, named after the KKK's first grand wizard, Nathan Bedford Forrest. If you live in South Carolina, you may drive down streets named after Confederate generals 'Stonewall' Jackson or Beauregard. Edmund Pettus Bridge, the historical bridge where blacks and whites were brutally assaulted by Alabama Security, is named after a Confederate general and the grand dragon of Alabama's Ku Klux Klan.

Yes, one can argue that this is part of our history and therefore we need to preserve these monuments and landmarks. And that is what history museums are for. Whether the Confederate flag is flying over a government building or a giant statue of Jefferson Davis is standing in a park in Memphis, they are honoring a long, dark tradition of racism and black inferiority.

Black history needs to be taught more thoroughly than it currently is in most schools. It is unacceptable to me that at the large, wealthy, predominantly white high school where I was formerly employed, has only a couple books about black history in its enormous library. It is unsatisfactory that United States history classes can be taught without mentioning the lynching of black Americans or the horrors of convict leasing. It is insufficient that the media is not discussing mass incarceration or the complete failure of the war on drugs with more frequency and detail.

In Germany it's a priority to inform the public about the horrors of the holocaust. "You cannot go to Germany, to Berlin, and walk 100 meters without seeing a marker or a stone or a monument to mark the places where Jewish families were abducted from their homes and taken to the concentration camps. Germans want you to go to the concentration camps and reflect soberly on the legacy of the Holocaust," says Bryan Stevenson.

Equal Justice Initiative is trying to erect landmarks of the domestic slave trade and of places where blacks were lynched in the South. They are trying to build awareness of the racial history that many of us are ignorant of. We need more of this. We need the people of the United States to understand the centuries of terror, humiliation, and injustice that Black Americans have experienced. If we want to change the biases and prejudices that we all have, it has to start with an adequate education of the history of racial injustices in the United States.

We cannot even begin to address the racial problems we currently have, without taking an honest look at our racial history. The racial injustices that African-Americans have endured cannot possibly be remedied until as a nation we admit to our legacy of white supremacy. Only then can we start to seek appropriate and long lasting remedies that will positively impact the lives of blacks. This is precisely what Republican congressman John Conyers has tried to accomplish by introducing bill H.R. 40: Commission to Study Reparation Proposals for African-Americans Act that "establishes the Commission to Study Reparation Proposals for African-Americans to examine slavery and discrimination in the colonies and the United States from 1619 to the present and recommend appropriate remedies."[160] But whenever the subject of reparations is brought up, it is quickly shot down as impractical and unrealistic.

But practicality of reparations is not the issue. The issue is that we are not interested in even exploring the plausibility of reparations in the United States. I am not going to dive into precisely how reparations would work. I am arguing that we need to be open to the idea. If this bill was passed, then we could begin to address the logistics of how it would work. Throughout this book, I have explained in great detail the plethora of injustices African-Americans have experienced in the last four hundred years in this country. Slavery, Jim Crow, lynching, convict leasing, housing discrimination, mass imprisonment, and police brutality give ample justification to provide African-Americans with some sort of meaningful reparations for their centuries of suffering at the hands of white supremacists and their sympathizers.

Reparations are possible. They have occurred before around the world and in the United States. The United States paid $20,000 to every Japanese-American who had been placed in a concentration camp during World War II. In "The Case for Reparations," Ta-Nehisi Coates describes West Germany's reckoning with its own dark past. After World War II, Israel started pushing for reparations for the atrocities committed at the hands of the Nazis. There was a strong and violent resistance by most Germans, who did not believe that Jews should receive anything. Some Germans even believed that Jews were at least partially responsible for the Holocaust. Violence ensued. Eventually West Germany agreed to pay Israel $7 million in today's US dollars.

"Individual reparations claims followed—for psychological trauma, for offense to Jewish honor, for halting law careers, for life insurance, for time spent in concentration camps. Seventeen percent of funds went toward purchasing ships," explains Coates. "Israel's GNP tripled during the 12 years of the agreement. The Bank of Israel attributed 15 percent of this growth, along with 45,000 jobs, to investments made with reparations money."

The psychological impact cannot be measured, but it surely went a long way to accomplish some kind of reconciliation. Reparations could never pay back the millions of families that lost loved ones in the Holocaust, just like reparations to African-Americans cannot undo the grave past, but they certainly are a step in the right direction. Reparations to African-Americans would not only go a long way in reducing the substantial wealth gap between whites and blacks, but also be an acknowledgment by the United States that we have a responsibility to own up to our past and help build a better future.

#

Building awareness and teaching history is a necessary step in the right direction, but it will not solve everything. The catastrophic effects the war on drugs has had on the United States, the world, and especially on poor people of color are astounding. To reverse these effects, the war on drugs does not need reform, it needs to end. There has been a growing number of acknowledgments by politicians, the media, and the public, that the war on drugs has been a complete failure. This is a positive sign.

However, upending the consequences of the war on drugs is no easy task. As the war on drugs has progressed throughout the last 40 years, it has become increasingly harder for politicians to speak out against the war on drugs. Being soft on crime has become tantamount to political suicide. Regardless of the obstacles that need to be overcome, politicians, lawyers, law enforcement, civil rights activists, and the general public need to come together and destroy the war, that has destroyed so many people's lives.

In Johann Hari's *Chasing the Scream*, he shows the repercussions the drug war has had on the world and the countries, states, and people who have made progress fighting it. He made me forever change the way I view drug addiction.

Hari says, "The opposite of addiction isn't sobriety. It's connection. Some 90 percent of people who use a drug—the overwhelming majority—are not harmed by it.... The unharmed 90 percent use in private, and we rarely hear about it or see it. The damaged 10 percent, by contrast, are the only people we ever see using drugs out on the streets. The result is that the harmed 10 percent make up 100 percent of the official picture."[161] To really understand what he means by this, we have to understand who uses drugs and why.

Studies have shown that drugs are most commonly used experimentally or occasionally by users; only a small percentage of drug users abuse drugs. So why then do only about 10 percent of people become addicted?

There is no one straight answer to this question. In fact, there are many reasons that people become addicted to drugs. One major reason is childhood trauma. In a detailed research study called the Adverse Childhood Experiences Study, scientists discovered that for each traumatic event a child experiences, are two to four times more likely to grow up to be an addicted adult. They claim nearly two-thirds of injection drug use is the product of childhood trauma.

The environment one lives in also has a tremendous influence on the likelihood that someone will become and stay an addict. For example, the indigenous people of North America were stripped of their land and their culture and collapsed into mass alcoholism.

The English poor were driven from farms to cities in the eighteenth century and turned to gin. After American inner cities lost factory jobs in the 1970s and 1980s, many of the unemployed turned to crack. The more rural Americans' markets and subsidies dried up, the more crystal meth usage increased.

The explosion of crack in the ghetto was a double whammy for inner city blacks. At one end, Reagan was using this as a political move to demonize blacks and expand the drug war. At the other end, crack came at a time where inner city blacks were vulnerable due to the extermination of most of their jobs. This hit particularly hard in Chicago's ghettos, especially Austin.

There are significant factors that lead to drug addiction beyond physical addiction to some substance. As a former personal trainer, I had obese clients that would come to me and want to lose weight. Some of these people were so obese that their life was in jeopardy. So, naturally, I created a workout routine to help them lose weight. I did not call the police and demand they be arrested for being obese. But this is exactly what has been happening during the war on drugs. Drug addicts are being thrown in jail and given long prison sentences for a sickness they have. And prison is the exact opposite of what they need.

If they are using drugs to cope with the trauma, self-hate, and loneliness, prison is only going to exacerbate the underlying issues of their drug abuse. Prison is the very epitome of isolation. It's no surprise then that when people are released from prison, they continue using or use even more. If you are one of those people that thinks drug and alcohol addicts are weak and deserve to be punished for their immoral and disgusting habits, then consider yourself lucky that, as Johann Hari says you never had to try and cope with more pain than you could bear.

It's not surprising that our society treats addicts as criminals when you consider that a person cannot visually see the internal pain that manifests in addicts. It is much easier to be compassionate, when we can see the ailment. Society would never look down on an amputee. It is unlikely that they would be denied treatment. But when we look at an addict out on the street, we do not feel the same compassion. We assume that they are living on the street because they want to be there or that they don't have the willpower to change. We need to start treating drug and alcohol addiction as a sickness, with compassion, and without judgment.

In the United States, we had a choice in how to deal with drugs. We could have gone with an approach exemplifying compassion and treatment or a punitive approach. We chose the latter. And this choice has come at a price. Since 1976 the war on drugs has cost more than $1 trillion and accounted for more than 45 million arrests. While it's possible to put a price on the amount of money the war on drugs has cost, it's not possible to put a price tag on the number of lives that the war on drugs has destroyed.

I'm not precisely sure what $1 trillion can buy; however, I know that if that money was used to treat addicts and other victims of the war on drugs, it could have saved many lives instead of destroying them. When faced with the dilemma of how to deal with the drug issue, Portugal chose this way. And it worked.

In the 1980s Portugal had one of the worst heroin addiction problems in the world. Initially, the government chose a route of criminalization and punishment. But the punitive approach was not working. In fact, drug problems were increasing. So Portugal decided to invest its money on educating children about drug abuse and provide treatment for addicts that focused on recovery. The Portuguese government also started giving tax breaks to employers that employ recovering addicts and decriminalized drugs. This does not mean that it was legal to sell drugs but it was no longer illegal to use and possess drugs. Portugal focused on the 10 percent of the population who were truly addicts, not the other 90 percent who used drugs recreationally.

Although the overall drug use went up slightly, the number of problematic drug users was cut in half, overdoses were reduced significantly, and the number of people contracting HIV through drug use fell from 52 percent to 20 percent. Additionally, there was a significant reduction in crimes directly related to drug use. Plus, police noted their relations with poor communities improved. At first decriminalization was very controversial in Portugal. Many politicians resisted the change. Now almost all of the Portuguese government is onboard with Portugal's drug policies because they have seen the overwhelming positive effects it has had in their country.

Johann Hari makes a strong argument for the legalization of drugs. This sounded crazy to me at first. How could heroin, meth, and crack be legalized? I encourage you to keep an open mind until you hear all the facts, then you can decide for yourself.

For one, legalization takes drugs out of the hands of gangs and criminals and puts it into the hands of the government. This alone would decrease drug and gang-related violence that we currently see around the world and in the inner cities of the United States. Al Capone would have had no business without Prohibition. Likewise, the Gangster Disciples would have no business without illegal drugs. And much of the crime that we see is a result of gangs trying to control land and the drug trade.

Hari explains that "when a popular product is criminalized, it does not disappear. Instead, criminals start to control the supply and sale of the

161

product. They have to get it into the country, transport it to where it's wanted, and sell it on the street. At every stage, their product is vulnerable. If somebody comes along and steals it, they can't go to the police or the courts to get it back. So they can only defend their property one way: by violence.... Professor David Nutt, the former chief scientific adviser to the British government on drugs published a study in *The Lancet,* Britain's leading medical journal, going through every recreational drug, and calculating how likely it was to harm you, and to cause you to harm other people. He found that one drug (alcohol) was quite far ahead of all the others. It had a harm score of 72. The next most harmful drug was heroin, and it had a harm score of 55, just ahead of crack at 54 and methamphetamine at 32. Smoking tobacco kills 650 out of every 100,000 people who use it, while using cocaine kills four."[162]

So even from a public health standpoint alcohol and tobacco are more harmful to people than heroin, crack, and meth. And alcohol and tobacco are legal. You may ask why the two drugs that cause more deaths than any other drugs are legal. The revenue generated by alcohol and tobacco make these two drugs way too profitable to criminalize.

Another question may arise: why should we legalize other drugs if alcohol and tobacco are already legal and they are causing so much damage? They are causing a substantial amount of damage, but this has nothing to do with the fact that they are legal. Other countries that have outlawed tobacco have not deterred their citizens from using it. People are going to use drugs whether they are legal or not. What does deter people from using drugs is a society that informs the public about the dangers of the drugs.

Hari describes the positive affects advertising against tobacco has had on public health: "As a result of this policy where tobacco is legal but increasingly socially disapproved of, cigarette smoking has fallen dramatically. In 1960 in the United States, according to the General Household Survey, 59 percent of men and 43 percent of women were smokers. Today, it's 26 percent of men and 23 percent of women - a halving. There have been similar trends across the developed world. Just because something harmful is legal doesn't mean people rush to use it: more and more are turning away from it."[163]

Next, let's use Amsterdam, the Netherlands, as an example. As many teenagers know, marijuana is legal in Amsterdam and has been for quite some time. So if legalization of drugs causes a spike in drug use, wouldn't Amsterdam have a high rate of pot users? Initially, the answer was yes, but over time the opposite was true. And the percentage of Dutch teenagers that have tried marijuana is lower than the number of American teens.

Surely the opposite trend would occur if more addictive drugs like heroin were legalized, right? Not exactly. Cities in Canada, Switzerland, and the United Kingdom experimented with clinics where trained professionals administered drugs to addicts. I assumed that if addicts could go into a clinic and have a nurse shoot them up with heroin for free, it would surely increase drug addiction. However, the facts show differently. According to Hari most addicts that were involved in this treatment simply stopped after around 10 years of use. The phenomenon is called maturing out or natural recovery.

Charles Winick, a psychologist that set up free clinics for addicts says they stop doing drugs because the "stresses and strains of life are becoming stabilized for them and because the major challenges of adulthood have passed."

By going to these clinics, addicts were not getting drugs that were laced with other harmful chemicals, like what they get on the street, but instead were getting pure drugs that were administered with sterile needles. They can also talk to medical professionals and address the underlying issues that are causing their addiction.

Most taxpayers would be outraged that the taxes they are paying are going to clinics that give addicts drugs for free. But it is much cheaper and effective to fund this kind of treatment versus the outrageous amount of money they already pay to enforce the war on drugs that is currently being waged. According to one estimate by the Cato Institute, legalizing drugs would save $41 billion a year currently spent in the United States on arresting, trying, and jailing users and sellers.

If the drugs were then taxed at a similar rate to alcohol and tobacco, they would raise an additional $46.7 billion a year, according to calculations by

163

Professor Jeffrey Miron of the Department of Economics at Harvard University. The money saved could be used to provide treatment and social reconnection for every drug addict in the United States.

Johann Hari created a list of pros and cons for legalizing drugs. His only con was that overall drug use will probably go up, but not tremendously. His list of pro's for legalization was much longer.

> Across the world, armed criminal gangs selling drugs will be financially crippled, from the Crips to the Zetas. The survivors will be pushed into much less profitable markets, where they will be able to do much less harm. As a result, the culture of terror that currently dominates whole neighborhoods and countries - from Brownsville, Brooklyn, to Ciudad Juarez - will gradually abate. (This happened after the end of alcohol prohibition). Enormous amounts of police time will be freed up to investigate other crimes. Trust in the police will begin to come back to poor communities. (This happened in Portugal).
>
> Teenagers will find it harder to get drugs. (This happened in the Netherlands). Overdoses will significantly decline, and the rate of HIV transmission will fall dramatically. (Both happened in Switzerland, the Netherlands, and Vancouver). The drugs people use will, in the main, be milder than today. (Remember the iron law and the end of alcohol prohibition). There will be a lot more money to spend on treating addicts and dealing with the underlying causes of addiction. Many addicts who currently get worse behind bars will get better in hospitals and then in new jobs. This means addiction will fall. (This happened in Portugal).
>
> Millions of people who are currently imposed for nonviolent offenses, at great expense to the taxpayers and to their communities, will walk free. Huge numbers of

African- American and Latino men who are currently locked out of the workforce, student loans, and public housing will be allowed back in. Shaming addicts will be replaced by caring for addicts."[164]

This is an overwhelming rational list that is supported by proof that legalization could and would work if it is approached correctly. Unfortunately, I do not see this happening in the United States. At least, not any time soon. We have made progress with the legalization of recreational marijuana in some states, but even this was a hard fought battle.

So without the decriminalization or legalization of drugs, how else can we diminish the consequences of the current state of the war on drugs? Laws, policies, and practices that have led to the decimation of poor communities need to end. Michelle Alexander says, "All of the financial incentives granted to law enforcement to arrest poor black and brown people for drug offenses must be revoked. Federal grant money for drug enforcement must end; drug forfeiture laws must be stripped from the books; racial profiling must be eradicated; the concentration of drug busts in poor communities of color must cease; and the transfer of military equipment and aid to local law enforcement agencies waging the drug war must come to a screeching halt."[165]

Without an end to the war on drugs, mass incarceration has no hopes of slowing down. The results of the war on drugs can be seen when entering any of the thousands of jails and prisons across the United States. According to Christopher Ingraham of the *Washington Post*, "We have slightly more jails and prisons in the US—five thousand plus—than we do degree-granting colleges and universities. In many parts of America, particularly the South, there are more people living in prisons than on college campuses."[166]

In her book *Incarceration Nations*, Baz Dreisinger states, "Money spent on prisons [in the US] has risen at six times the rate of spending on higher education; it costs $88,000 per year to incarcerate a young person, more than eight times the $10,653 to educate her."[167]

The outcome of the prison-industrial complex has been devastating to this country, the states, and cities within it, and most of all the poor communities of color and the people living in them.

Maya Schenwar states, "Conversations, correspondences, and relationships with prison-torn families have taught me that separation breeds more separation, that the coldness and isolation of prison breed the coldness and isolation of violence. And I think about how the one-on-one relationship, in which the prisoner emerges as a person (with thoughts, a personality, a history, hopes, dreams, nightmares), might serve as a model for the beginning of a person-based, connection-based justice system."[168]

So essentially, confining millions of people to isolation only exacerbates the issues prisoners are originally imprisoned for. In the captivating movie *Shawshank Redemption*, Andy Dufresne, played by Tim Robbins, says, "The funny thing is, on the outside, I was an honest man, straight as an arrow. I had to come to prison to be a crook."

It would be one thing if prisons have actually been proven to work. We could possibly justify jails and prisons as a necessary evil if they deterred crime and made our neighborhoods safer. Dreisinger notes, "Prison populations in America have grown steadily since 1973 and do not correlate whatsoever with crime rates.... Studies in probability theory and psychology reveal that deterrence is an illusion. Few people stop committing crimes because prison exists; the reality of its existence hardly factors into their thought process while criminal acts are occurring."[169]

Even in countries where horrific punishments are issued to criminals, crimes are committed nonetheless. A 2014 report from the National Research Council concluded that more severe sentences do not effectively deter crime.

Michelle Alexander adds, "Imprisonment now creates far more crime than it prevents, by ripping apart fragile social networks, destroying families, and creating a permanent class of unemployables.... Although it is common to think of poverty and joblessness as leading to crime and imprisonment ...the war on drugs is a major cause of poverty, chronic unemployment, broken

166

families, and crime today.... As a crime reduction strategy, mass incarceration is an abysmal failure. It is largely ineffective and extraordinarily expensive.... Racial impact statements that assess the racial and ethnic impact of criminal justice legislation must be adopted. Public defender offices should be funded at the same level as prosecutor's offices to eliminate the unfair advantage afforded the incarceration machine."[170]

These are very realistic solutions that can be administered with just a little thought and effort.

The termination of the current cash bail system is also essential in eliminating the unjust treatment of the poor. People without the money to pay for bail are profoundly disadvantaged when compared to people who have the means to pay. Maya Schenwar cites, "A study of people in New York City arrested on non-felony charges whose bail was set at $1,000 or less showed that 87 percent were in jail because they could not pay the bail amounts.... Those who are jailed while awaiting trial are more likely to be convicted and more likely to receive long sentences than their bailed-out counterparts, who are able to address their legal charges from within their communities. Plus, people who are jailed before trial may lose their jobs, housing, or custody of their children—and may feel forced to accept a plea bargain just to get out temporarily."[171]

So based on an individual's economic status, they will either get to await trial in the comfort of their home, or they will await trial in the harsh conditions of a jail. Some organizations have been developed to pay for the bail of people who cannot afford it. These organizations try to get the individual drug treatment if needed or adequate attorneys that can help with their case. Some organizations are also advocating release and community accountability instead of cash bail. If cash bail is not altogether ended, then more organizations like this are needed to address the unfair consequences facing poor people, usually of color.

When it comes to crime and punishment, the mentality in the United States has always been one of revenge and brutality. We have an odd obsession with the necessity to inflict as much harm as possible on people who have done wrong. The answer to the question of how to reduce crime has always resulted in an increase of punishment. Solitary confinement, long sentences, and capital punishment have become increasingly normalized in the eyes of our criminal justice system. These punishments affect minorities and especially blacks at much higher rates. The United States stands with a motley crew of countries that still practice the death penalty. Most of these countries being ruthless authoritarian regimes that have very little freedom. In fact, America is the only Western country in the world that still executes its citizens. Here in the United States, we proudly proclaim we are the land of the free, while prisoners rot in isolated boxes at alarming rate. We declare that we are home to the most just society in the world, yet we execute more people than any other First World country. We need not to become numb to these barbaric practices, but work towards a criminal justice system that is simultaneously just and effective.

Our justice system has become disturbingly successful in punishing the perpetrators of crimes, but has not concerned itself proportionately with the victims of these crimes. There needs to be more prominence on how the perpetrator and the state can help the victim recover and less of an emphasis on how to punish the offender. Simply punishing the offender is not a solution to the crime they committed. It is not aiding the victim and at the same time is creating a cycle of revenge, where no progress is being made on either end. I am not advocating a lack of accountability for the perpetrator of the offense, just pointing out that we should not excessively punish the offender while ignoring the victim.

Baz Dreisinger explains that restorative justice can be beneficial for the victim of a crime, who needs answers, empowerment, restoration of respect, and restitution. This is usually most effective by means of some kind of dialogue between the offender and the victim. The victim can then begin contemplating the idea of forgiveness. And then, true healing can occur when the victim no longer is consumed with hate and revenge. They can then start to rebuild the brokenness that the offender has created. In this process, the offender can take ownership of their acts, and start to come to terms with how they are going to make reparations to the victim.

When crimes are committed, we need not to go straight to the most punitive measure. We should consider other approaches. It may be foreign to us in this country, but in many European countries only a small percentage of those convicted are sentenced to prison.

Dreisinger explains, "The Netherlands, where courts are required to give special reasons whenever a custodial sentence is ordered instead of a fine, uses 'transactions'-by which a person who commits a crime pays the treasury or fulfills financial conditions or participates in a training course-and 'task penalties,' reminiscent of Rwanda's TIG sentences, involving a work order that benefits the community."[172]

In situations where an individual commits a violent crime and is deemed too dangerous to society, they should attend some type of facility where they can receive real rehabilitation, not a place where they will continue to deteriorate to the point in where the damage is irreversible. A place where they can begin to address their deep rooted anger without the constant threat of violence.

It is said that prevention is the best medicine. Indeed, it is difficult to treat cancer once it has already developed, but we have learned that there are many things we can do to lower our chances of getting cancer. Like in the medical field, a criminal justice system that makes prevention a priority is critical to reduce mass incarceration. Money should be allocated more towards preventative measures that will decrease future crime.

Implementing programs in and out of school that allow kids to gain the tools they need for employment should be part of the plan. Giving our youth more opportunities to be involved in productive activities like sports, art, and music clubs will give them a meaningful distraction from the crime and despair that is widespread in poor neighborhoods. Mentoring programs that assign at risk children with good role models is productive and meaningful. Punitive measures that tear poor communities apart, should be replaced with programs that bring communities together.

Reforming laws and policies that make recidivism so common are also a step in the right direction. Allowing felons better access to housing and jobs would help reduce the high rate of recidivism. Empowering communities to participate in programs that help felons successfully reintegrate into society is a more productive way than sending ex-convicts back to prison for minor parole violations, which only increases the never ending cycle of poverty and crime. Allowing fathers to be part of their kids' lives instead of making children grow up without parental guidance, will help deter kids from making the same mistakes as their parents.

The recidivism rate in the United States is about 60 percent. This means that only about 40 percent of ex-prisoners do not return to jail or prison. I am stating the obvious by exclaiming that 40 percent is a very low success rate. If only 40 percent of students at a particular school were graduating, the school would be shut down. If a business is successful only 40 percent of the time, it would close. So why, then, are we not moving to a more productive approach?

The prison-industrial complex is so big and lucrative that it has created a great investment to build private prisons. We are building more and more new prisons, and these prisons have to be filled. So laws and policies have to ensure that these prisons are filled. Not only are they being filled, but it is more profitable to overcrowd them, leading to a deterioration of conditions inside jails and prisons. Phone companies, gun manufacturers, and health care providers also have big stakes in prisons. Phone companies profit from charging families of prisoners ridiculously high amounts. Gun manufacturers profit from selling Tasers and guns to prisons. Healthcare providers profit from giving prisoners abysmal health insurance. Many companies save money from the products prisoners produce when incarcerated. More and more people are being employed within the prison-industrial complex, also complicating the issue of reigning in this profitable beast.

Despite this monster that we have built, the support for mass incarceration has been dwindling recently. Even Republicans are coming to terms with the fact that it does not work, and we need to go in a different direction. This is a good sign, yet it will take an extraordinary effort to bring significant and long lasting change. The powers that be will have to realize that its citizens no longer will tolerate a system that is so unjust and detrimental. And this can only be done by fundamentally changing the way we think about criminal justice and then act on it.

#

Another crucial solution to the current state of black lives is police reform. The tension between the police and black communities is perhaps the most noticeable in today's society. We have all seen the pictures and videos of police brutality. We then have witnessed the ensuing protests, rioting, and looting across urban America. We all have our opinions on who to hold responsible. Some of us believe the police are to blame, and others condemn criminals and the Black Lives Matter movement. What is clear, however, is that change is necessary.

After the killings of Michael Brown and Freddie Gray and the resulting riots in Ferguson and Baltimore, the police have encountered a tremendous amount of criticism. Some of this criticism is fair and some is not. To put all of the blame on law enforcement regarding the escalation of the war on drugs and the rise of the prison-industrial complex is not fair or accurate. As discussed in depth, the laws and policies put in place by eager politicians to prove their toughness on crime, has resulted in the police being obligated to follow suit. This created an us vs. them mentality. Much of law enforcement view the people they are supposed to be protecting with contempt and aggression, and many people in poor communities see the police not as their protectors but as an invading army. The mistrust many people in these neighborhoods feel towards the police creates a dangerous environment where many people take the law into their own hands.

In Jill Leovy's incredible book *Ghettoside*, she explains:

> Many critics complain that the criminal justice system is heavy-handed and unfair to minorities. We hear a great deal about capital punishment, excessively punitive drug laws, supposed misuse of eyewitness evidence, troubling high levels

of black male incarceration, and so forth. So to assert that black Americans suffer from too little application of the law, not too much, seems at odds with common perception. But the perceived harshness of American criminal justice and its fundamental weakness are in reality two sides of a coin, the former a kind of poor compensation for the latter. Like the schoolyard bully, our criminal justice system harasses people on small pretexts but is exposed as a coward before murder. It hauls masses of black men through its machinery but fails to protect them from bodily injury and death. It is at once oppressive and inadequate."[173]

This is, indeed, a strange concept. How can blacks in ghettos have too much policing and not enough at the same time? We have already discussed the over-criminalization of blacks in regards to drugs and other nonviolent offenses, but isn't it strange that despite this overwhelming police presence, it minimally affects black-on-black violence?

Blacks have always been targeted by the police for the most insignificant offenses. Hortense Powdermaker, who was a Jim Crow era anthropologist, noted, "The Southern legal system of the 1930s hammered black men for such petty crimes as stealing and vagrancy, yet was often lenient toward those who murdered other blacks. In Jim Crow Mississippi, killers of black people were convicted at a rate that was only a little lower than the rate that prevailed half a century later in Los Angeles."[174]

With the exception of the last couple of decades, most highly publicized cases of blacks who were killed by the police, and black-on-black violence in inner cities received almost no media attention. Even today, black-on-black violence in inner city ghettos rarely receives much more than a footnote on the nine o'clock news. Every once in a while there will be a notable amount of publicity generated by a very young black kid getting shot by a stray bullet, or a dedicated black cheerleader who was on the honor roll getting caught in the crosshairs of gang violence.

However, young black men who are murdered due to gang violence get little acknowledgment by the corporate media. They are all assumed to be ruthless gang members and therefore, apparently, undeserving of recognition or sympathy. A young black male living in the inner city who is murdered will in all likelihood not receive the same amount of attention by law enforcement that a white girl in a wealthy suburb will be granted. Partly because law enforcement in poorer neighborhoods are preoccupied fighting the war on drugs and partly because they have less resources and motivation to apprehend the killers.

Changing the us versus them police culture can help build trust between police officers and the communities they serve. In *Rise of the Warrior Cop*, author Radley Balko, explains what real community policing means.

> Taking cops out of patrol cars to walk beats and become a part of the communities they serve. It means ditching statistics- driven policing, which encourages the sorts of petty arrests of low-level offenders and use of informants that foment anger and distrust.... Police today are also given too little training in counseling and dispute resolution, and what little training they do get in the academy is quickly blotted out by what they learn on the street in the first few months on the job. When you're given an excess of training in the use of force but little in using psychology, body language, and other non-coercive means of resolving a conflict, you'll naturally gravitate toward force....
> Legislatures should pass laws that not only clearly establish a citizen's right to record on-duty cops but provide an enforcement mechanism so that citizens wrongly and illegally arrested have a course of action.[175]

Balko also says that police officers that are in good physical condition have also been proven to be less likely to use lethal force.

Other possible solutions include mandatory data collection for police and prosecutors to eliminate selective enforcement. Requiring police departments to report officer shootings and use of excessive force to an independent federal agency. Only using SWAT teams in extraordinary situations like hostage situations. Records of judges and search warrants should be publicly accessible to heighten transparency.

The police are currently a protected class. They are essentially above the law they are supposed to be enforcing. Police officers have the same unwritten law that criminals have: don't snitch on your own.

> In numerous states across the country, police unions have lobbied legislatures to pass variations on a law enforcement bill of rights. Though they vary from state to state, the general thrust of these laws is to afford police officers accused of crimes additional 'rights' above and beyond what regular citizens get.... These laws have made it nearly impossible to fire bad cops in many jurisdictions, and worse, they have instilled in them the notion that they're above the law - and above the regular citizens they're supposed to serve.... under the qualified immunity from civil lawsuits currently afforded to police under federal law, a police officer can't be sued for mere negligence - or even for gross negligence that results in a fatality.[176]

If we want to experience real justice in the United States, the police have to be held to the same standards as its citizens, and because they are not, the public has to demand police accountability. The recent protests and riots against police brutality around the country are proof that the public can make a difference if they come together.

Residents in high crime areas need to be proactive and collaborate together to take pressure off the police. I am not advocating, like many politicians, that more fathers need to be around, and that poor communities just need to pull themselves up by their bootstraps. I understand the structural and systemic issues that make this impossible. I am simply advocating that communities come together and help one another out. Disadvantaged neighborhoods with higher levels of trust and communication among neighbors have lower crime rates.[177]

As difficult as it is to stand up to gangs, the power of numbers can be a great equalizer. When the innocent, nine-year-old Tyshawn Lee was lured into an alley and murdered in retaliation against the boy's father, the public should have demonstrated the same anger and support as when Laquan McDonald was murdered by police officer Jason Van Dyke. We need to be outraged by all murders and rally behind the families of victims to reduce the likelihood of similar tragedies from happening again.

#

Economic inequality shows no signs of slowing down in the United States or around the world. This inequality is exceptionally apparent between whites and blacks in the US and is a major concern for all Americans says Matt Taibbi's in his book, *The Divide.*

> [The US still has] the superficial characteristics of a functional free democracy. Underneath the surface is a florid and malevolent bureaucracy that mostly (not absolutely, but mostly) keeps the rich and the poor separate through thousands of tiny, scarcely visible inequities....We have a profound hatred of the weak and the poor, and corresponding groveling terror before the rich and successful, and we're building a bureaucracy to match those feelings.... Since 2008, no high-ranking executive from any financial institution has gone to jail, not one, for any of the systemic crimes that wiped out 40 percent of the world's wealth.... For most of the poor people who are being sent away, whether it's for a day or for ten years, their prison lives begin when they're jailed for the most minor offenses imaginable.[178]

Despite all of the success the United States has experienced, in many respects, the divide between black and white Americans and the poor and the rich, has been expanding. Blacks have created their own culture based on the isolation and segregation of many communities. North Lawndale—a poor, crime- ridden neighborhood slightly to the Southeast of Austin Village—is more segregated now than it was when Martin Luther King lived there in 1966. Despite attempts from the Occupy Movement, economic inequality has continued to grow in the United States. According to Joseph E. Stiglitz, author of *The Price of Inequality* and winner of the Nobel Prize, the United States not only has the highest level of inequality among the advanced industrial countries, but the level of its inequality is increasing in absolute terms relative to that in other countries. If we want to make the United States a better country for everyone, we seriously need to address the social, racial, and economic inequality that is permeating through this country.

In response to the riots that sparked after the assassination of Martin Luther King, Jr., President Lyndon Johnson formed the 11-member Kerner Commission in hopes to understand the cause of the riots and how to prevent more in the future. In a report given by the Kerner Commission, they stated, "Our nation is moving toward two societies, one black, one white—separate and unequal."

Despite the periodic progress that has been made, I think it is accurate to say that we are not anymore moving to two separate societies, but moved. This is evident by the extreme concentration of African-Americans living in inner city and some suburban and rural areas. The invisible wall that divides Oak Park from Austin illustrates this division.

Andrew Hacker, the author of *Two Nations*, notes, "Black Americans are Americans, yet they still subsist as aliens in the only land they know. Other groups may remain outside the mainstream—some religious sects, for example— but they do so voluntarily. In contrast, blacks must endure a segregation that is far from freely chosen. So America may be seen as two separate nations. of course, there are places where the races mingle. Yet in most significant respects, the separation is pervasive and penetrating. As a social and human division, it surpasses all others—even gender—in intensity and subordination."[179]

Segregation of public facilities may have ended a long time ago, but residential segregation is very much still alive. In fact, many cities and towns are more segregated now than when segregation was legal over fifty years ago. We now have neighborhoods on the West and South Sides of Chicago that are over 98 percent black. And because of the low mobility in these poor black neighborhoods, these residents most likely never come into contact with white people, or anyone other than blacks for that matter. The kids that populate these hyper-segregated neighborhoods grow up without knowing other cultures and races. Likewise, whites that live in sundown towns that have very few or no black residents have the same problems. This type of isolation breeds closed mindedness and racist ideals. It allows stereotypes and misconceptions to control their thinking. It fosters a dehumanizing effect that is placed on people we don't know or understand. Not to mention all of the unequal opportunities that residents have depending on the neighborhood that they inhabit. This is why during the *Brown vs. Board of Education* legal battle, it was said that separate facilities are inherently unequal. Getting to know different cultures and types of people expands our knowledge and allows us to dispel myths we once perceived of other cultures, races, and religions. Having neighborhoods where there is more equality gives equal opportunities for all residents.

Residential segregation is a tough egg to crack. Even Dr. King could not break down the walls of segregation in the North. Whites are more resistant to blacks living in their neighborhoods than any other form of segregation. It is also misleading and inaccurate to believe the common misconception that blacks live and stay in black areas because of preference and comfortability. It is undoubtedly true that some African-Americans prefer to live in black neighborhoods, but it is not the consensus. This type of thinking also denies the issues that led to segregated communities, such as widespread housing discrimination and the prevalence of sundown towns.

So how do we change this? The Gautreaux Project in Chicago proved to be beneficial. This project, which gave prior residents of public housing vouchers to live in nicer suburbs, was largely successful. Most former public housing tenants who resided in the ghetto adapted very well when living in more affluent metropolitan areas.

Research suggests that being exposed to new surroundings had transforming effects on the families placed in white neighborhoods, with more children graduating from high school and half going on to college. Black parents in suburbia were also much more likely than parents in inner cities to find work in the suburbs. Similar programs were then implemented in other cities across the US, most of which experienced the same successful results.

In his book *Evicted*, Matthew Desmond echoes the importance of voucher programs and suggests they be used as a universal program.

> Every family below a certain income level would be eligible for a housing voucher. They could use that voucher to live anywhere they wanted, just as families can use food stamps to buy groceries virtually anywhere, as long as their housing was neither too expensive, big, and luxurious nor too shabby and run-down. Their home would need to be decent, modest, and fairly priced. Program administrators could develop fine-grained analysis, borrowing from algorithms and other tools commonly used in the private market, to prevent landlords from charging too much and families from selecting more housing than they need. The family would dedicate 30 percent of their income to housing costs, with the voucher paying the rest
>
> Vouchers are far more cost-effective than new construction, whether in the form of public housing or subsidized private development" (Evicted, 309). Desmond explains that a "universal voucher program would change the face of poverty in this country. Evictions would plummet and become rare occurrences. Homelessness would almost

disappear. Families would immediately feel the income gains and be able to buy enough food, invest in themselves and their children through schooling or job training, and start modest savings. They would find stability and have a sense of ownership over their home and community.[180]

This is a simple, realistic approach that is very plausible and cost-effective. It is not that we do not have the resources to provide a program like this; it's that we lack the desire.

James Loewen suggests enacting what he calls a Residents' Right Act, which can help decrease residential segregation in this country.

> This law provides that in counties with an unusual disparity between the percentage of the black and white electorates registered to vote, the Department of Justice can send in federal examiners, once complaints have been received from ten individuals who were rebuffed when trying to register.... He goes on, "a blatant disparity between the percentage of a town's population that is African-American compared to the proportion in the metropolitan area) the entire state for independent sundown towns) will trigger sanctions under the Residents' Rights Act - when coupled with at least two valid complaints from families who were rebuffed when trying to buy or rent a home in the community and a careful showing that it was a sundown town.[181]

Desegregating towns in the United States may be difficult, but it is possible. If the false perceptions that residents in predominantly white neighborhoods have of blacks change, towns will be more welcoming to the arrival of new black residents. If the untrue stereotypes of blacks bringing down property values and deteriorating neighborhoods is met by educated individuals who resist this type of harmful exclusion, there will be less exclusion from whites. Oak Park is a great example of a community that is devoted to fair housing.

As noted before, Oak Park has not always been the racially inclusive place it is currently. Today, however, Oak Park has the reputation of being one of the most racially inclusive and diverse neighborhoods in the Chicago area. This is no accident. In 1970 Oak Park was less than 1 percent African-American, but this started to change as the decade progressed. By 1980, Oak park was about 11 percent African-American, and this trend continued throughout the next decades. Today, Oak Park is about a quarter African-American. So how then did Oak Park go from a sundown town to one of the most racially inclusive areas in the Chicago Metropolitan area?

In the 1960s and 70s, Austin changed from a mostly white neighborhood to a predominately black, segregated area. Oak Park soon began to open housing agencies in order to both change their community into a more inclusive place and to prevent a complete resegregation, like what was occurring just east of Austin Boulevard.

Oak Park residents decided that they were going to proactively promote racial inclusion in their neighborhood. Organizations such as the Oak Park Housing Authority, the Oak Park Residence Corporation, and the Oak Park Regional Housing Center committed to ensuring that Oak Park would be a town that carried out fair housing practices. They offered, and still offer, affordable housing options to low-income families, provide federal rent subsidies, and discourage steering.

The commitment to dispersing African-Americans evenly throughout Oak Park has been instrumental in avoiding areas that are high in racial concentration. Many towns may not show the same racism and discrimination that created much of the segregation that now persists, but they are not proactively making their communities more diverse either. Oak Park has not maintained neutrality, like other complacent towns. They have created an atmosphere and reputation that encourages racial diversity and inclusion. More towns need to follow their lead.

If you truly believe that the United States government, without provocation, will make the necessary changes that are needed to end the oppression of the marginalized poor, you're kidding yourself. We need only to look back in time to see who really instigated positive change. It was activists like Frederick Douglass, Harriet Tubman, John Brown, and thousands of others who created a movement that led to the abolition of slavery. It was the relentless work of W.E.B Dubois and Ida. B. Wells who forced anti-lynching legislation to be implemented. It was Martin Luther King, Jr., SNCC, CORE, and many other civil rights activists who dictated the legislation that ended segregation and other discriminatory practices during the Civil Rights Era.

It will inevitably take a similar revolution by the public to affect the deep- rooted inequality that is currently evident in the United States. To end the war on drugs, mass incarceration, and other forms of racial, social, and economic inequality, a mass movement needs to be created by the general public. For this to happen, people need to start caring about the injustices that occur daily in the United States.

In *This is an Uprising*, Mark and Paul Engler give examples of the major impacts that nonviolent revolts have, and continue to have, on the world. They discuss everything from the uprisings that Mohandas Gandhi led to free his people from British colonial rule, to the uprising in Serbia, to the crusade that Martin Luther King led right here in America.

They state that contrary to what most people believe and how the media portrays nonviolent revolts, "those who practice it tell us that outbreaks of widespread disruption, although commonly misunderstood, are neither flukes nor fleeting failures. Rather, they are forces that can be guided with the exercise of conscious and careful effort.... Time and again, in uprisings that steal the spotlight and illuminate injustices that are otherwise ignored, we see three elements-disruption, sacrifice, and escalation-combining in forceful ways."[182]

They discuss the meticulous planning, organizing, and strategies involved in nonviolent revolts. They explain that most revolts that we see on TV may seem to be spontaneous, but when dissected more closely, they are the result of deliberate strategies, many which have been proven effective before. The Englers explain that nonviolent movements that are founded on certain principles can be very influential in changing public opinion, which in turn, changes societies. These movements do not make changes overnight, but with the right strategy, discipline, and persistence, over time, can and do make significant and long lasting change.

Benjamin Franklin once said that, "Justice will not be served until those who are unaffected are as outraged as those who are." Truer words have never been spoken. The people who are affected the most by injustice, are the same people who do not have the political and economic influence to create drastic change. This does not mean that these people cannot make meaningful change. They can and do, with the right strategy and organization.

Just look at the impacts that the Black Lives Matter movement has made. The demonstrations in Ferguson, Baltimore, and others throughout the US have made a tremendous impact on the accountability of police officers. Even though some of the rioting and looting has been counterproductive, most demonstrations have been non-violent and overall, have been sufficiently productive. Many people perceive Black Lives Matter activists as an unorganized, impulsive group. But the Black Lives Matters organization is a legitimate group that is organized with realistic and appropriate goals.

The countrywide activism against police brutality is working. It is leading to more police accountability. It is highly unlikely that if it wasn't for the activism and the videotaping of the police, that this kind of change would have been possible. In fact, it is likely that all or most of police indictments in recent years would have been covered up instead. The victims most likely would have never received any justice, and the public may have never even been informed.

Michelle Alexander, Radley Balko, and Johann Hari all echo the urgency for the public to take an active role in forcing policymakers and politicians to make changes. Michelle Alexander says that without a fundamental shift in public consciousness, the system as a whole will remain intact. Radley Balko believes bad systems will remain in effect until policymakers and politicians decide it is more politically expedient to acknowledge and address the problem. And Johann Hari says being part of a community makes people less vulnerable. Mark and Paul Engler state that most social advancement is the result of political movements. Nonviolent action is paramount in creating the change we so desperately need. Everyone needs to start caring like they are affected by these injustices. Because we are all affected. Maybe not directly. But as US citizens, we are all responsible for creating a more just society. A society where all human beings are treated with dignity and respect. A country where everyone receives equal rights regardless of religion, class, or race.

Conclusion

There is a strength, a power even, in understanding brokenness, because embracing our brokenness creates a need and desire for mercy, and perhaps a corresponding need to show mercy. When you experience mercy, you learn things that are hard to learn otherwise. You see things you can't otherwise see; you hear things you can't otherwise hear. You begin to recognize the humanity that resides in each of us. ~ Bryan Stevenson

Divided only by a street, Oak Park and Austin are two radically different places. In David Shipler's book, A Country for Strangers: Blacks and Whites in America, he describes the invisible wall that separates Oak Park and Austin.

"A line runs through the heart of America. It divides Oak Park from Chicago's West Side along the stark frontier of Austin Boulevard, splitting the two sides of the street into two nations, separating the carefully integrated town from the black ghetto, the middle class from the poor, the swept sidewalks from the gutters glistening with broken glass, the neat boutiques and trim houses from the check-cashing joints and iron-grilled liquor stores."22

Today, Austin is about 85% black and less than 5% white. The few white and Latino residents that do live in the neighborhood tend to occupy their own enclaves within Austin, now the second largest of the 77 Chicago neighborhoods.

The poverty level in Oak Park is below 9 percent and in Austin it is more than 35 percent. About 96 percent of Oak Park residents are high school graduates, but only 75 percent of Austin residents have obtained their high school diploma. The median household income of Oak Park residents is almost $79,000, but in Austin it is barely $32,000. The crime in these two communities can hardly be compared because they are so vastly different.23

Austin's decline began prior to the arrival of African-Americans in the mid-1960s. A lot of the buildings and roads were old and needed updates. The white residents of Austin had long been advocating for the improvement of infrastructure in their neighborhood, but the West Side has never had the political power of other parts of the city. As blacks arrived in Austin, they entered an area that had long been neglected. This neglect was exacerbated as whites fled the area. As whites dispersed to other areas, jobs and businesses followed them and left Austin. To make matters worse, African-Americans lived in over priced homes that needed maintenance. Without the money to pay for this maintenance, housing deteriorated and property values lowered. Schools became overcrowded and inadequate. Many Chicago Public Schools went to a schedule where students would only attend school for a half of a day, leaving kids roaming the streets in their spare time. Riots broke out in Austin High School due to the racial tension that was so prevalent in Austin and throughout the United States during this time. After Martin Luther King Jr. was assassinated, riots ensued and Chicago burned for days. The West Side was hit particularly hard, losing millions of dollars in damage. Many of the buildings that were decimated during this time were never repaired.

As jobs began to go overseas, African-Americans suffered disproportionately as they made up a large part of this kind of industrial labor. Due to all these factors, gangs, drugs, and violence wreaked havoc on Austin and other West Side neighborhoods. Areas like Austin became increasingly vulnerable during the 1970s and 80s as heroin and crack entered inner city neighborhoods across the United States. Desperate and jobless, many inner city residents turned to gangbanging and selling drugs to make quick money and to fill the void in their lives. As the War on Drugs and the militarization of the police escalated, neighborhoods like Austin were devastated. In 2011, Adams Street in Austin became the most incarcerated block in Chicago. When those who have been incarcerated get out, they often go back to neighborhoods like Austin, where they are discriminated against and fall back into the same patterns that landed them in prison in the first place, perpetuating this never ending cycle.

As the housing crisis and Great Recession tore through American neighborhoods, Austin would not escape its wrath. Unemployment and underemployment increased and residents were targeted disproportionately with subprime loans, leading to high foreclosure rates and vacant buildings throughout the neighborhood. Austin currently faces the highest amount of foreclosures of any neighborhood in the city. Rahm Emanuel's decision to close down over 50 schools in Chicago affected kids and families in Austin tremendously. Four Chicago Public Schools were closed in Austin and currently, most high school aged students living in Austin attend school outside of the Austin area. A local high school in Austin, Frederick Douglass Academy High School, continues to lose enrollment and there have been rumors of its impending closure.

The population in Austin continues to decline as residents are moving out of the area in hopes of finding an area that can offer better jobs, schools, stores, and less violence. Other residents are determined to stay and keep fighting to help Austin achieve the potential they envision for the community. I also see this potential and will continue to fight for Austin.

#

As I drive on Austin Boulevard and through Austin today (two years later), my perceptions have changed. I am at complete ease as I cruise through Austin with one hand on the steering wheel and the other out the window. I am not drenched in sweat. I do not feel like I am going to get attacked, robbed, or shot.

In a way, this is strange. Before I lived on Austin Boulevard, I had never been in Austin before, and I was completely ignorant of what went on there. For instance, I did not know that just a few years ago, a street in Austin was the most incarcerated street in all of Chicago. I was ignorant of the fact that a certain gang controlled a street I regularly travel on. I was unaware that there was a shooting at the very intersection that I usually catch a red light on my way to work, just a few nights before.

Despite all of this, I still feel relatively safe as I drive through Austin Village on my way to work and back home. I used to think that I was at a higher risk because I was white. But now I know that the majority of people living in Austin are hardworking, compassionate people. I know because I have come to know many of these people. I have never been attacked, robbed, or witnessed a shooting or robbery. My car and apartment have never been

186

vandalized and nothing has ever been stolen from them. In fact, I once lost my wallet on the green line in Austin and someone contacted me and returned my wallet with everything intact.

So where did I get these ideas that I could never go into Austin?

Growing up in a predominately white suburban neighborhood has a lot to do with my misconceptions. As a kid I heard stories about inner city neighborhoods. I had never actually known anyone from one or even stepped inside one. I constantly heard and watched stories on the news of black people in these neighborhoods killing and robbing each other. My family, friends, and strangers always cautioned me to never go near these neighborhoods. Not because they were racist, but because they believed the same things that I used to believe. All of my thoughts and perceptions about communities like Austin were negative because that's what I heard. Not until I actually lived on Austin Boulevard and got to know people living in Austin Village, did my perceptions begin to change. And not until I educated myself on black history, did I understand how Austin developed into what it currently is.

Even though, my perceptions of Austin have changed for the better, I still realize the struggles that people living there face. It is a fact that Austin is a dangerous neighborhood to live in. Austin has gangs, crime, poverty, and an extreme lack of resources to overcome them. There are few jobs, unhealthy restaurants (if you consider Church's Chicken, Dunkin Donuts, and McDonald's restaurants), vacant and dilapidated houses, high levels of police surveillance, guns, drugs, the list goes on and on. These are, in fact, all the more reasons people need to help. And Austin Village is merely one small example of a plethora of other communities that experience similar issues.

In Bryan Stevenson's moving book, *Just Mercy*, he expresses that he has "come to believe that the true measure of our commitment to justice, the character of our society, our commitment to the rule of law, fairness, and equality cannot be measured by how we treat the rich, the powerful, the privileged, and the respected among us. The true measure of our character is how we treat the poor, the disfavored, the accused, the incarcerated, and the condemned. We are all implicated when we allow other people to be mistreated."[183]

187

As a society how does our character measure up to these standards? In my opinion, not very well. In the United States, we reward the rich and powerful and punish the poor and weak. Those with enough money or power can act with almost complete impunity. They can obtain the best lawyer that money can buy who they can work with in the leisure of their home when they post bail. They can lobby for laws that ensure their way of living will not be tampered with. They can thrust our economy into a depression and walk away scot-free. They can invest in an economy that supports the destruction of the climate and world as we know it. They can do all these things, but yet they cannot provide us with universal health care or adequate paid annual and maternity leaves. The rich can insure their privacy by purchasing acres of land and high tech security systems, but the poor can be subjected to unwarranted harassment at the whim of the authorities. We can find the money to fund our never ending wars, but we cannot cease from being the country with the highest poverty rate amongst all industrialized nations. Billionaires can fly around in their private jets at will, but yet the US has the lowest social mobility out of any industrialized country.

So, where do we go from here? In short, we need to start caring. We have to change into a society where we value people, not things. A society where all people have worth, not just the privileged. We have an obligation to morph into a society that values and exhibits mercy, compassion, and justice. Bryan Stevenson puts it this way: "Mercy is most empowering, liberating, and transformative when it is directed at the undeserving. The people who haven't earned it, who haven't even sought it, are the most meaningful recipients of our compassion."

We cannot simply turn a blind eye to neighborhoods like Austin. We have to give the voiceless a voice, the weak strength, the uneducated an education, and the condemned a chance. We should replace our ignorance with knowledge, our judgments with education, our prejudices with compassion, and our hate with love. But more than anything, we need to leave our comfortable, cozy lives, and start fighting to make a difference.

Afterword

A few months ago, I was asked to attend an event located at Columbus Park in the Austin Community about bridging the gap between Austin and Oak Park. The Oak Park Regional Housing Center and Austin Rising, who organized the event, suggested that we refer to the whole area of Oak Park and Austin as the Greater West Side. Referring to the area as the Greater West Side would hopefully be a step in the right direction in trying to reduce the stigma of the division that exists between the two communities. As Oak Park and Austin residents discussed the division between the two neighborhoods, most agreed that the narrative about Austin needs to change.

I have discussed the many challenges facing Austin and similar communities throughout this book. We need to be realistic about the inequities that exist in Austin, but we should not only focus on the negative. Focusing only on the crime and gangs portrays an inaccurate and misleading picture of the Austin community. It perpetuates negative stereotypes that create more walls than bridges. We also need to talk about the assets that already exist in Austin. There are countless organizations, activists, churches, and residents that are making a real difference in the area. There are historic, beautiful houses within the Austin limits. Although there is a significant level of poverty in the community of Austin, there are many residents that are well off and have many resources. Many of these residents live in Austin Village, which is an unofficial part of Austin, near the town hall.

As we try to change the narrative about Austin, we should also have a realistic view of Oak Park. Oak Park is perceived as a utopian paradise where the races intermingle effortlessly. Oak Park is nationally famous for its level of integration, but we should not use this as a justification to be complacent about the work that still needs to be done. When Barack Obama became the 44th President of the United States, there were many people claiming that we had entered a post-racial society. This color-blind mentality has opened the door for new ways of discrimination. When talking to people about my book, countless people have said something to the effect that "Oak Park is not as open and accepting as its reputation claims." While Oak Park is a great community, it needs to confront its own racial divisions. Residents do and should continue to change the perceptions about Austin, and try to make both communities more inclusive and just places to live.

As politicians use racial fear mongering and other tactics in an attempt to divide us for their own political motivations, we should realize that we are more similar than different. Whether we are black or white, rich or poor, live in Austin or Oak Park, all people want the same things. We all strive for safe communities, good schools, affordable housing, trustworthy neighbors, local entertainment, and everything else that contribute to vibrant communities. The sooner we can change our mindset, the closer we get to breaking down barriers like Austin Boulevard.

Jeff Ferdinand
August, 2017

Notes

Invisible Wall

[1] Katie Kather, "Austin Boulevard: The Invisible Barbed Wire," https://katiekather.atavist.com/story/6737

[2] http://www.encyclopedia.chicagohistory.org/pages/93.html

[3] Isabel Wilkerson, *The Warmth of Other Suns: The Epic Story of America's Great Migration*. New York: First Vintage Books Edition, 2011

[4] Wilkerson, 179

[5] Ibid, 15

[6] Ibid, 418

[7] Ibid, 262-63

[8] Anna Layson and Kenneth Warren. "Chicago and The Great Migration, 1915-1950." *The Newberry*. http://dcc.newberry.org/collections/chicago-and-the-great-migration

[9] Wilkerson, 270

[10] Ibid, 277

[11] Ibid, 372

[12] Ibid, 297

[13] Ibid, 297

[14] Ibid, 273

[15] Ibid, 376

[16] Loewen W. James, *Sundown Towns: A Hidden Dimension of American Racism,* New York: First Touchstone Edition, 2006, 4

[17] Ibid, 12

[18] Ibid, 59

[19] Ibid, 258

[20] Ibid, 128, 133

[21] Ibid, 218

[22] David Shipler, *A Country for Strangers: Blacks and Whites in America.* [23] http://www.city-data.com/Oak-Park-Illinois.html, http://www.census.gov/quickfacts/table/PST045215/1754885,1714000

America's Peculiar Institution

[24] Michelle Alexander, *The New Jim Crow: Mass Incarceration in the Age of Colorblindness*, New York: The New Press, 2012, 25.

[25] James and Lois Horton, *Slavery and the Making of America*, 26

[26] Ibid, 107

[27] Edward Baptist, *The Half Has Never Been Told*, xxi

[28] Edmund Morgan, *American Slavery, American Freedom*, 23

[29] Ibid, 57-58

[30] Baptiste, xix

[31] Howard Zinn, *A People's History of the United States*, 26

[32] Ibid, 32

[33] Horton, 93

[34] Ibid, 115

[35] Horton, 115

[36] James McPherson, *Battle Cry of Freedom,*

[37] James W. Loewen, *Lies My Teacher Told Me,* 141-42

[38] Dred Scott v. Sandford, 60 US 393 1857,

[39] Oswald Garrison Villard, *John Brown: A Biography*

Freedom?

[40] Horton, 174-175

[41] Ibid, 175

[42] Ibid

[43] Leon F. Litwack, *Been in the Storm So Long,* 81

[44] Ibid, 128

[45] Ibid, 97-98

[46] Litwack, 103

[47] Zinn, 191

[48] Litwack, 183

[49] Ibid, 195

[50] Ibid, 139

[51] Ibid 125

[52] Ibid, 129

[53] Ibid, 120-30

[54] http://www.history.com/topics/american-civil-war/reconstruction

[55] Douglas Blackmon, *Slavery by Another Name,* 25

[56] Litwack, 276

[57] Ibid, 278

[58] Ibid, 258

[59] Ibid, 262-63

[60] Ibid, 285

[61] Ibid, 284

[62] Ibid, 284

[63] Ibid, 279

[64] Philip Dray, *At the Hands of Persons Unknown,* 51

[65] *Slavery by Another Name,* 47.

[66] Ibid 57

[67] Ibid 96

[68] Ibid 62.

[69] Ibid 121.

[70] Ibid

[71] Ibid51, 333.

[72] Ibid 56

[73] Ibid 307.

[74] Ibid, 318.

[75] Ibid319.

[76] Ibid364

[77] Phillip Dray At The Hands of Persons Unknown, ix.

[78] At The Hands of Persons Unknown, x.

[79] Ibid, pictures.

[80] Ibid xi

[81] Ibid, 55.

[82] Ibid, 54.

[83] Blackmon, 110

[84] Ibid, 157

[85] Ibid, 121-122

[86] Ibid, 106

[87] The Strange Career of Jim Crow, 97

[88] Ibid, 98

[89] Ibid, 99.

[90] Ibid, 99-100.

[91] Ibid, 101.

[92] Ibid, 102.

[93] At The Hands of Person's Unknown, 198.

[94] The Strange Career of Jim Crow, 113

[95] Ibid, 114

[96] Ibid 10, 12, 159-60

[97] Ibid, 167

[98] Ibid, 173

[99] Ibid, 175

[100] Henry Hampton and Steve Fayer, *Voices of Freedom*, 19

[101] The King Years, 24

[102] Hampton and Fayer Voices of Freedom, 124.

[103] Voices of Freedom, 124

[104] Diane McWhorter in *Carry Me Home* 39

[105] Voices of Freedom, 133

[106] Hampton and Fayer Voices of Freedom, 137.

[107] http://www.history.com/topics/black-history/freedom-summer

[108] Johann Hari Chasing the Scream, 294

The Windy City

[109] Isabel Wilkerson, The Warmth of Other Suns, 386

[110] Beryl Satter, Family Properties, 170

[111] Family Properties, 40

[112] Ibid.

[113] Satter Family Properties, 37

[114] Family Properties, 46

[115] Ibid, 46

[116] Ibid, 176

[117] Ibid, 190

[118] Ibid, 196

[119] Ibid, 199

[120] Ibid, 212

[121] James Loewen Sundown Towns, 354

[122] Family Properties, 331

[123] Matthew Desmond, Evicted, 75

[124] Kevin Boyle Arc of Justice, 9-10

[125] Ghetto, 11

[126] Evicted 4, 98

[127] Ibid, 252

The War on the Poor, The Rise of the Military Industrial Complex

[128] The New Jim Crow, 48
[129] Kristian Williams, *Our Enemies in Blue*, 148
[130] The New Jim Crow, 52
[131] Ibid, 75
[132] Radley Balko, *Rise of The Warrior Cop*, xii
[133] The New Jim Crow, 85
[134] Ibid
[135] Locked Down Locked Out, 30, 45
[136] The New Jim Crow, 106-7
[137] Chasing the Scream, 54
[138] Chris Hedges Wages of Rebellion, 111
[139] The New Jim Crow, 253

The Five-O

[140] Wages of Rebellion, 146-147
[141] Our Enemies in Blue, 70
[142] Ibid, 128
[143] Ibid, 150, 165
[144] Ibid, 131
[145] Ibid, 135
[146]http://www.washingtonpost.com/sf/investigative/2015/04/11/thousands-dead-few-prosecuted,
[147] Sarah Macaraeg and Alison Flowers, Who do you Serve, Who do you Protect? 36

Mythbusting

[148] American Apartheid, 162
[149] "Welfare Queen' Becomes Issue in Reagan Campaign." New York Times. 1976- 02-15. p. 51
[150] Zinn, 579
[151] Harriet Washington, Medical Apartheid, 58
[152] Medical Apartheid, 45
[153] Khalil Gibran Muhammad, the author of *The Condemnation of Blackness*, 20- 21
[154] A Country of Strangers, 286-287
[155] The Condemnation of Blackness, 76
[156] At The Hands of Persons Unknown, 95
[157] Sundown Towns, 38

Solutions

[158] http://www.eji.org/racepoverty/racialinjustice
[159] http//www.themarshallproject.org/2015/06/24/bryan-stevenson-on- charleston-and-our-real-problem-with-race?edium=social&utm_campaign=sprout&utm_source=facebook
[160] https://www.congress.gov/bill/113th-congress/house-bill/40

[161] Chasing the Scream, 147, 293

[162] Ibid, 54, 183

[163] Ibid, 262

[164] Ibid, 272

[165] The New Jim Crow, 232-233

[166] http://www.washingtonpost.com/news/wonkblog/wp/2015/01/06/the-u-s-has-more-jails-than-colleges-heres-a-map-of-where-those-prisoners-live/

[167] Incarceration Nations, 15

[168] Locked Down, Locked Out

[169] Incarceration Nations, 17

[170] The New Jim Crow, 23-237

[171] Locked Down Locked Out, 126

[172] Incarceration Nations, 292-3

[173] Jill Leovy *Ghettoside*, 9

[174] Ghettoside, 9

[175] Rise of the Warrior Cop, 325, 327

[176] Ibid, 328-329

[177] Evicted, 70

[178] The Divide, xxi-xxii, xxiv

[179] Two Nations, 3

[180] Evicted, 308-9

[181] Sundown Towns, 442

[182] This Is an Uprising, 284

[183] Bryan Stevenson, *Just Mercy*

Bibliography

Ackerman, Spencer. "'I Sat in That Place for Three Days, Man': Chicagoans Detail Abusive Confinement Inside Police 'Black Site.'" *The Guardian*, February 27, 2015. https://www.theguardian.com/us-news/2015/feb/27/chicago-abusive-confinment-homan-square.

Alexander, Michelle. *The New Jim Crow: Mass Incarceration in the Age of Colorblindness*. New York: The New Press, 2012.

Balko, Radley. *The Rise of the Warrior Cop: The Militarization of America's Police Forces*. New York: Public Affairs, 2013.

Baptist, Edward E. *The Half Has Never Been Told: Slavery and the Making of American Capitalism*. Perseus Books Group, 2015.

Baum, Dan. *Smoke and Mirrors: The War on Drugs and the Politics of Failure*. Boston: Brown, Little, 1996.

Bellware, Kim. "Chicago Cop Who Killed Rekia Boyd Quits, Preserving His Cushy Retirement." *The Huffington Post*, May 17, 2016. http://www.huffingtonpost.com/entry/dante-servin-quits_us_573b7f22e4b0ef86171c6575.

Plutarch. "The Life of Solon" in *Lives of the Noble Greeks and Romans*.

Blackmon, Douglas A. *Slavery by Another Name: The Re-Enslavement of Black Americans from the Civil War to World War II*. New York: Anchor Books, 2009.

Boyle, Kevin. *Arc of Justice: A Saga of Race, Civil Rights, and Murder in the Jazz Age*. New York: Henry Holt and Company, 2004.

Branch, Taylor. *The King Years: Historic Moments in the Civil Rights Movement*. New York: Simon & Schuster, 2013.

Brown v. Board of Education of Topeka, 347 U.S. 483 (1954).

Caputo, Angela. "Cell Blocks." *The Chicago Reporter*, March 1, 2013.

"Causes of the Civil War." *HistoryNet*. http://www.historynet.com/causes- of-the-civil-war.

Choldin, Harvey M. "Chicago Housing Authority." In *Encyclopedia of Chicago,* edited by Janice L. Reiff, Ann Durkin Keating, and James R. Grossman. Chicago Historical Society, 2005. http://www.encyclopedia.chicagohistory.org/pages/253.html.

Coates, Ta-Nehisi. *"The Case for Reparations."* *The Atlantic,* June, 2014. http://www.theatlantic.com/magazine/archive/2014/06/the-case-for- reparations/361631.

Desmond, Matthew. *Evicted: Power and Profit in the American City.* New York: Crown Publishing Group, 2016.

Dray, Philip. *At the Hands of Persons Unknown: The Lynching of Black America*. New York: Modern Library, 2003. Paperback edition.

Dred Scott v. Sandford, 60 US 393 (1857).

Dreisinger, Baz. *Incarceration Nations: A Journey to Justice in Prisons Around the World*. New York: Other Press LLC, 2016.

"Drug War Today." *TheHouseILiveIn.com*. Accessed September 5, 2016, http://www.thehouseilivein.org/get-involved/drug-war-today.

Duneier, Mitchell. *Ghetto: The Invention of a Place, the History of an Idea*. New York: Farrar, Straus, and Giroux, 2016.

Editorial Board. "Editorial: Rekia Boyd shooting was 'beyond reckless,' so cop got a pass." Chicago Tribune, April 22, 2015. http://www.chicagotribune.com/news/opinion/editorials/ct-cop-verdict-servin-edit-0423-20150422-story.html.

Eltagouri, Marwa. "Austin population drops to No. 2 in city for first time in 45 years." Chicago Tribune, July 14, 2017.

Engler, Mark, and Paul Engler. This is an Uprising: How Nonviolent Revolt is Shaping the Twenty-First Century. New York: Nation Books, 2016.

Equal Justice Initiative. "A History of Racial Injustice." http://www.eji.org/racepoverty/racialinjustice

Franklin, Tim, and William B. Crawford Jr. "County OKs Panther Death Settlements." *Chicago Tribune*, November 2, 1982.

"Freedom Summer." *History.com*. 2009. http://www.history.com/topics/black-history/freedom-summer.

Friedersdorf, Conor. "The Number of Cops Indicted for Murder Spikes Upward." *The Atlantic*, August 19, 2015. http://www.theatlantic.com/politics/archive/2015/08/the-shocking- number-of-cops-recently-indicted-for-murder/401732.

Goodman, Amy, David Goodman, and Denis Moynihan. *Democracy Now!: Twenty Years Covering the Movements Changing America*. New York: Simon & Schuster, 2016.

Gray, Mike. *Drug Crazy: How We Got into This Mess & How We Can Get Out*. New York: Random House, 1998.

Hacker, Andrew. *Two Nations: Black and White, Separate, Hostile, Unequal*. New York: Macmillan, 1992.

Hampton, Henry, and Steve Fayer. *Voices of Freedom: An Oral History of the Civil Rights Movement from the 1950s through the 1980s*. New York: Bantam Books, 1990.

Hari, Johann. *Chasing the Scream: The First and Last Days of the War on Drugs*. New York: Bloomsbury Books, 2015.

Hedges, Chris, and Joe Sacco. *Days of Destruction Days of Revolt*. New York: Nation Books, 2014.

Hendricks, Kasey, Amanda E. Lewis, Ivan Arenas, and Deana G. Lewis. A Tale of Three Cities: The State of Racial Justice in Chicago Report. Institute for Research on Race and Public Policy. Chicago, 2017.

Horton, James O. and Lois E. Horton. *Slavery and the Making of America*. New York: Oxford University Press, 2006.

http://www.city-data.com/Oak-Park-Illinois.html

http://www.census.gov/quickfacts/table/PST045215/1754885,1714000

Ingraham, Christopher. "The U.S. has more jails than colleges. Here's a map of where those prisoners live." *The Washington Post*, January 6, 2015.
http://www.washingtonpost.com/news/wonkblog/wp/2015/01/06/the-u-s- has-more-jails-than-colleges-heres-a-map-of-where-those-prisoners-live.

Johnson, Corey G. "Bryan Stevenson on Charleston and Our Real Problem with Race." *The Marshall Project*, June 24, 2015. https://www.themarshallproject.org/2015/06/24/bryan-stevenson-on-charleston-and-our-real-problem-with-race? utm_medium=socialHYPERLINK

Kather, Katie. "Austin Boulevard: The Invisible Barbed Wire." https://katiekather.atavist.com/story/6737.

Kerner Commission. "Report of the National Advisory Commission on Civil Disorders." Washington: U.S. Government Printing Office, 1968.

Khalek, Rania. "Unarmed Black Woman Shot and Killed by Chicago Police Officer Less Than a Month After Trayvon Martin Shooting." *Truthout*, April 6, 2012. http://www.truth-out.org/news/item/8308-unarmed-black- woman-shot-and-killed-by-chicago-police-officer-less-than-a-month-after- trayvon-martin.

Kimberly, Kindy, and Kelly Kimbriell. "Thousands Dead, Few Prosecuted." *Washington Post*, April 11, 2015. http://www.washingtonpost.com/sf/investigative/2015/04/11/thousands- dead-few-prosecuted.

King, Gilbert. *Devil in the Grove: Thurgood Marshall, the Groveland Boys, and the Dawn of a New America*. New York: HarperCollins, 2012.

Krist, Gary. *City of Scoundrels: The 12 Days of Disaster That Gave Birth to Modern Chicago*. New York: Random House, 2012.

Layson, Anna, and Kenneth Warren. "Chicago and the Great Migration, 1915- 1950." *The Newberry*. http://dcc.newberry.org/collections/chicago-and-the- great-migration.

Leovy, Jill. *Ghettoside: The True Story of Murder in America*. New York: Spiegel and Grau, 2014.

Lincoln, Abraham. *The Collected Works of Abraham Lincoln (Volume 8, 1864-1865)*, edited by Roy P. Basler. New Brunswick, NJ: Rutgers University Press, 1988.

Litwack, F. Leon. *Been in the Storm So Long: The Aftermath of Slavery*. New York: Vintage, 1980.

Loewen, James W. *Lies My Teacher Told Me: Everything Your American History Textbook Got Wrong*. New York: First Touchstone Edition, 1996.

Loewen, James W. *Sundown Towns: A Hidden Dimension of American Racism*. New York: First Touchstone Edition, 2006.

Malcolm X. "Message to Grassroots." November 9, 1963.

Malcolm X. Speech at Audubon Ballroom in Harlem. December 13, 1964.

Martin, Judith A. "Austin." In *Encyclopedia of Chicago*, edited by Janice L. Reiff, Ann Durkin Keating, and James R. Grossman. Chicago Historical Society, 2005. http://www.encyclopedia.chicagohistory.org/pages/93.html.

Massey, S. Douglas and Nancy A. Denton. *American Apartheid: Segregation and the Making of the Underclass*. Cambridge, London: Harvard University Press, 1998.

McPherson, James M. *Battle Cry of Freedom: The Civil War Era*. Oxford, England: Oxford University Press, 1988.

McWhorter, Diane. *Carry Me Home: The Climactic Battle of the Civil Rights Revolution*. New York: Simon & Schuster, 2002. First Touchstone edition.

Miller, Michael E. "Cop accused of brutally torturing black suspects costs Chicago $5.5 million." *Washington Post*, April 15, 2015.

https://www.washingtonpost.com/news/morning-mix/wp/2015/04/15/closing-the-book-on-jon-burge-chicago-cop-accused- of-brutally-torturing-african-american-suspects.

"The Montgomery Bus Boycott." *History.com*, 2010. http://www.history.com/topics/black-history/montgomery-bus-boycott.

Morgan, S. Edmund. *American Slavery, American Freedom: The Ordeal of Colonial Virginia*. New York: Norton, 1975.

Muhammad, Khalil Gibran. *The Condemnation of Blackness: Race, Crime, and the Making of Modern Urban America*. Cambridge: Harvard University Press, 2011. Paperback edition.

Nixon, Richard. "Remarks About an Intensified Program for Drug Abuse Prevention and Control." June 17, 1971. http://www.presidency.ucsb.edu/ws/?pid=3047.

Oak Park Housing Authority. http://www.oakparkha.org/

Oak Park Residence Corporation. http://www.oakparkrc.com/

Padgett, Ken. "Blackface!" *Minstrel Shows*. http://black-face.com/minstrel- shows.htm.

Petty, Audrey, ed. *High Rise Stories: Voices from Chicago Public Housing*. San Francisco: Voice of Witness, 2013.

"Reconstruction." *History.com*. 2009. http://www.history.com/topics/american-civil-war/reconstruction.

Satter, Beryl. *Family Properties: How the Struggle Over Race and Real Estate Transformed Chicago and Urban America*. New York: Picador, 2009.

Schenwar, Maya. *Locked Down, Locked Out: Why Prison Doesn't Work and How We Can Do Better*. Oakland: Berret-Koehler, 2014.

Schenwar, Maya, Joe Macare, and Alana Yu-lan Price. *Who Do You Serve, Who Do You Protect?: Police Violence and Resistance in the United States*. Chicago: Haymarket Books, 2016.

Seligman, Amanda I. Block by Block: Neighborhoods and Public Policy on Chicago's West Side. Chicago: The University of Chicago Press, 2005.

"Separate is Not Equal: Brown vs. Board of Education." *Smithsonian National Museum of American History*. http://americanhistory.si.edu/brown/history/5-decision/courts-decision.html.

Shawshank Redemption. Film. Directed by Frank Darabont. West Hollywood, CA: Castle Rock Entertainment, 1994.

Shipler, David K. *A Country of Strangers: Blacks and Whites in America*. New York: Knopf, 1997.

Shipler, David K. *Arab and Jew: Wounded Spirits in a Promised Land*. New York: Penguin, 2002.

Stevenson, Bryan. *Just Mercy: Story of Justice and Redemption*. New York: Spiegel and Grau, 2014.

Stewart, John. *The Daily Show*. June 18, 2015.

Stiglitz, Joseph E. *The Price of Inequality: How Today's Divided Society Endangers Our Future*. New York: W. W. Norton & Company, 2013.

Taibbi, Matt. *The Divide: American Injustice in the Age of the Wealth Gap*. New York: Spiegel & Grau, 2014. Trade paperback edition.

The Anti-Inauguration: Building resistance in the Trump era. Chicago: Haymarket Books, 2017.

The Daily Take Team. The Thom Hartmann Program, Op-Ed. "Food Stamps Are Affordable; Corporate Welfare is Not." *Truthout*, November 5, 2013. http://www.truth-out.org/opinion/item/19844-food-stamps-are-affordable- corporate-welfare-is-not.

The Oak Park Regional Housing Center. http://www.liveinoakpark.com/

Villard, Oswald Garrison. *John Brown, 1800-1859*. Philadelphia: Williams Brothers, 1872.

Washington, A. Harriet. *Medical Apartheid: The Dark History of Medical Experimentation on Black Americans from Colonial Times to the Present*. New York: Anchor, 2008. Reprint edition.

Wiesel, Elie. "Have You Learned The Most Important Lesson Of All?" May 24, 1992. Parade Magazine.

Wilkerson, Isabel. *The Warmth of Other Suns: The Epic Story of America's Great Migration*. New York: Vintage, 2011.

Williams, Kristian. *Our Enemies in Blue: Police and Power in America*. Oakland, Edinburg, Baltimore: AK Press, 2015. Third edition.

Woodward, C. Vann. *The Strange Career of Jim Crow*. Oxford: Oxford University Press, 1974. Third revised edition.

Zinn, Howard. *A People's History of the United States*. New York: Harper Perennial, 2005.

Made in the USA
Middletown, DE
14 March 2018